社会科学
研究文库

索我理想之中华

——中国留学生之父容闳图传

徐惠萍◎著

南方传媒　广东人民出版社

·广　州·

图书在版编目（CIP）数据

索我理想之中华：中国留学生之父容闳图传 / 徐惠萍
著. —广州：广东人民出版社，2023.12
ISBN 978-7-218-17325-2

Ⅰ. ①索… Ⅱ. ①徐… Ⅲ. ①容闳(1828—1912)—传记
Ⅳ. ①K827＝6

中国国家版本馆 CIP 数据核字（2024）第 010865 号

SUO WO LIXIANG ZHI ZHONGHUA——ZHONGGUO LIUXUESHENG ZHI FU RONGHONG TU ZHUAN
索我理想之中华——中国留学生之父容闳图传

徐惠萍　著　　　　　　　　　　　　　　　　　版权所有　翻印必究

出 版 人：肖风华

责任编辑：梁　茵　陈泽航
封面设计：奔流文化
责任技编：吴彦斌

出版发行：广东人民出版社
地　　址：广州市越秀区大沙头四马路 10 号（邮政编码：510199）
电　　话：(020) 85716809（总编室）
传　　真：(020) 83289585
网　　址：http://www.gdpph.com
印　　刷：珠海市豪迈实业有限公司
开　　本：787 毫米×1092 毫米　1/16
印　　张：17.5　字　　数：200 千
版　　次：2023 年 12 月第 1 版
印　　次：2023 年 12 月第 1 次印刷
定　　价：98.00 元

如发现印装质量问题，影响阅读，请与出版社 (020-85716849) 联系调换。
售书热线：(020) 87716172

总　序

党的十八大以来，习近平总书记围绕构建中国特色哲学社会科学提出一系列新主张新论述新要求，作出了一系列重大部署。2016年，习近平总书记在哲学社会科学工作座谈会上指出："一个没有发达的自然科学的国家不可能走在世界前列，一个没有繁荣的哲学社会科学的国家也不可能走在世界前列。坚持和发展中国特色社会主义……哲学社会科学具有不可替代的重要地位。"党的二十大报告强调："深入实施马克思主义理论研究和建设工程，加快构建中国特色哲学社会科学学科体系、学术体系、话语体系，培育壮大哲学社会科学人才队伍。"2023年10月，习近平文化思想的正式提出为新时代哲学社会科学事业创新发展、谋篇布局指明了方向，提供了科学指南和根本遵循。

珠海经济特区成立四十多年来，始终坚持解放思想，深化改革，扩大开放，始终担负起中国改革开放和现代化建设排头兵、先行地、试验区的职责使命，取得了举世瞩目的巨大成就。珠海市哲学社会科学界坚持用习近平新时代中国特色社会主义思想凝心铸魂，聚焦珠海经济社会发展的理论和现实问题，不断推动哲学社会科学的知识创新、理论创新、方法创新，陆续推出系列理论阐释的时代力作、咨政建言的智慧成果、服务人民的学术精品，先后编辑出版了《珠海潮》和《珠海社科学者文库》，为汇集高质量哲学社会科学研究成果，激发社科工作者研究热情，促进哲学社会科学事业繁荣进步，服务珠海高质量发展作出了积极贡献。

进入新时代，珠海迎来了前所未有的发展机遇，粤港澳大湾区、横琴粤澳深度合作区、自由贸易试验区、现代化国际化经济特区"四区"叠加，一系列重大机遇相互促进、相互推动、相互彰显，释放出强大的发展潜力，珠海的地位、方位、定位达到了前所未有的高度。时代的呼唤，形势的发展，对珠海哲学社会科学事业的发展提出了新的更高要求。为进一步引领和激励广大哲学社会科学工作者紧紧围绕珠海经济社会发展开展更深层次的研究，充分发挥"思想库""智囊团"作用，打造高水平社科成果品牌，2023年，珠海市社科联对原有《珠海社科学者文库》进行优化提升，推出《珠海社会科学研究文库》，集中出版最新理论研究成果和新型智库研究成果，为构建具有珠海特色的哲学社会科学体系搭建了平台，全市哲学社科界将以此为契机，继续深入理论研究，深入基层，贴近一线，多出精品，多出力作，为珠海走在全面建设社会主义现代化国家前列贡献社科智慧和力量，开创新时代珠海哲学社会科学事业发展新局面。

《珠海社会科学研究文库》编审委员会

2023年12月

索我理想之中华

Striving for My Ideal China

——中国留学生之父容闳图传

A Pictorial Biography of Yung Wing

容闳（1828.11.17-1912.4.21）

族名达萌，号纯甫，英文名Yung Wing

有些人注定是为时代而生的，他们在某一个特定的时间点横空出世，影响并推动那个时代。容闳就是这样的人。随着15世纪开始的地理大发现、新航路的开辟以及欧洲殖民主义者的全球扩张，人类第一次建立起跨越大陆和海洋的全球性联系。遥远东方一个叫做澳门的小岛，成为古老帝国融入全球化的起点。而容闳就出生在与澳门一箭之遥的地方，他注定成为那个时代的弄潮儿。作为最早留学美国的先行者，他不仅是中国百年留学大潮的开启者，而且他设计和推动的清政府第一次官派留美运动，为中国近代化的转型播下了火种。

Some individuals are born for their era, emerging at a specific point in time to influence and propel it forward. Yung Wing was such a person. He not only inaugurated the century-long trend of Chinese studying abroad but also planted the seeds of transformation for China's modernization by spearheading the Qing's first official delegation of Chinese students to America.

～ 本书作者 ～

徐惠萍，毕业于中国新闻学院，担任过新华社记者，报社总编辑，长期致力于对容闳的研究，撰稿并策划纪录片《容闳》在中央电视台纪录片频道播出，获中国影视大奖提名奖、广东省第十届精神文明建设"五个一工程"优秀作品奖，著有书籍《先行者容闳》。

～ 本书英文翻译 ～

黄植良（Sam Jake Leong Wong）
黄智珏（Evelyn Zhi Jue Wong）
黄植良毕业于耶鲁大学，与黄智珏同为邝其照后代。邝其照是第一个编写汉英词典的中国人，容闳好友，清廷第四批留美幼童领队。黄植良在国内外刊物上发表多篇相关学术文章，如《晚清观察家及其对排华法案的影响》《〈广报〉在晚清民族主义宣传和改革思想传播中的作用》等。

目 录
contents

前 言

以图证史

雷 颐

　　与惠萍相识近二十年了，我在北京研究中国近代史，她在珠海从政，一南一北，职业不同，本无任何交集，但诞生于香山，也就是今天珠海的容闳，成为我们相识的媒介，二十年来，成为至友。

　　本人长期从事中国现代化转型、中西文化交流史研究，容闳是一位作用重要、必须重视的先驱性人物。容闳诞生于珠海，无疑是珠海的骄傲，是珠海一张明亮的"名片"，推动容闳研究、宣介容闳事迹、弘扬容闳精神，是珠海文宣部门义不容辞的责任。惠萍曾是珠海文宣部门的领导，对此工作自然尽心尽责，甚至用殚精竭虑形容也不为过。不知不觉，惠萍为容闳的精神和人格所吸引，虽然工作变动且于几年前退休，有关容闳的种种事务与她已全然无关，但她一直想方设法继续推动容闳研究、宣介容闳事迹、弘扬容闳精神。不仅如此，她在知命之年竟然开始独立研究，著书立说，写下自己对容闳的感佩和见解。对她而言，尽心尽责殚精竭虑推动有关研究、宣介、弘扬工作，已从一种外在的"职务行为"内化为自己内心深处的一种"召唤"（calling），"职业"成为自己的"志业"。1917年秋，德国著名社会学家、哲学家马克斯·韦伯发表了影响深远的演讲《学术作为一种志业》，将"职业"与"志业"区分开来，"职业"是为了生存的"稻粱谋"，而"唯有发自内心对学问的献身，才能把学者提升到他所献身的志业的高贵与尊严"。惠萍对"容闳事业"的热爱与激情，提升了自己的高贵、尊严与境界。

　　多年来，惠萍潜心悉心搜集有关容闳的大量资料，几年前出版了《先行者容闳》，获得好评。现在她以搜集到的大量图片为基础推出《索我理想之中华——

中国留学生之父容闳图传》（以下简称《容闳图传》），另有一番意义。

在文字发明前，图画是人类最早传递、记录信息的符号；文字发明后，千百年来文字几乎成为记载历史、保存记忆的唯一工具，但摄像技术的发明，使文字的这种功能开始面对挑战。摄影是工业社会对政治、历史和大众生活最有影响的发明之一，其触角从宏大的社会、政治场景一直伸展到普通人生活的最私密部分。它将稍纵即逝的种种"场景"摄取、保存下来，使之进入"历史"、成为对过去"记忆"的最重要"证据"之一。纪实照片以其"形象逼真"受到空前的重视，"影像"逐渐成为与"文字"一样重要的记载历史、保存记忆的工具。它甚至还能通过人物无意识的瞬间表情，深入到人的心灵深处，正如瓦尔特·本雅明在《摄影小史》中所说："我们即便能顺畅而大概地描述人类如何行走，却一点也不能分辨人在一秒瞬间迈开步伐的真确姿态是如何。然而，摄影有本事以放慢速度与放大细部等方法，透露了瞬间行走的真正姿势。只有借着摄影，我们才能认识到无意识的视像，就如同心理分析使我们了解无意识的冲动。"

《容闳图传》将有关容闳的图片汇集一处，形成"整体性冲击"。更难得的是，这些图片都附有详细的文字说明，恰如本雅明所说："相机会愈来愈小，也会愈来愈善于捕捉浮动、隐秘的影像，所引起的震撼会激发观者的联想力。这里，一定要有图说文字的介入，图说借着将生命情境作文字化处理而与摄影建立关系，少了这一过程，任何摄影建构必然会不够明确。"详细的图片说明使一幅幅原本孤立的图片、一个个凝固的瞬间突然更具内在联系性，突然连贯起来。图像与文字之间的这种关系，更是不同文本间的"对话"，彼此互为"语境"，互相诠释、加深对方的意义。图文一体，读者如同乘船航行在一条缓缓流淌的时间长河上，历史画面在两岸依次展现。这种非连续性与连续性之间，形成了读者的体会、感悟、思考历史的空间。

　　然而，如果选图不当或文字说明不当，图与文将"分裂独立"、意义互损。如何选图怎样撰文，考验着作者的眼光、学识与水平。《容闳图传》选图精当，文字准确简明，图与文成为一种互动互补的张力关系，相得益彰，图像和文字组合加深甚至创造了一种新的意义空间，使受众生成了一种新的阅读感受，不仅使读者对容闳和近代中国的感受、理解更加直观、生动、强烈，而且更加深刻。在这图文并茂后面，深藏着惠萍对容闳和珠海的热爱，体现了她"所献身的志业的高贵与尊严"。

2023年11月8日于北京

（本文作者系中国社会科学院近代史所研究员，著名历史学家）

守书犹见照灯痕

——为《容闳图传》作记

苏炜

那是2011年盛夏的深圳，我正陪同一位耶鲁音乐指挥参与一场为世界大学生运动会献演的大型音乐会。暌违多年的一位中山大学老学弟辗转找到旅馆见我，奉上他珍藏多年的一本容闳出版于1909年的英文自传《西学东渐记》的初版英文本——*My Life in China and America*，恳请我在此珍本的扉页上题上几句话。我怀着虔敬的心情，信笔写下——

有幸成为容闳先辈的耶鲁传人，我任教耶鲁迄今已十数载矣。"容闳"的名字是我在课堂上重复频率最高的中文姓名。容闳此书的中译篇名《西学东渐记》之"西学东渐"，也是我在授课中要求学生记诵的中国现当代史的关键字之一。今天看到这本初版和原版的《西学东渐记》，有一种抚弄故人手泽的温润感和仰止之情。记得我常常在校园内向过往旅人指点介绍哪一栋楼、哪一扇窗曾染上过容闳的灯火，今天这灯火就在手上的这本珍本上持续燃烧，并将燃烧永远。

匆匆又是十余年过去。今天（2023年初夏），在耶鲁澄斋（我的办公室雅号）高窗透映的朝阳下，我又有幸亲炙这部《索我理想之中华——中国留学生之父容闳图传》。掀篇的第一句话就让我感怀不已——"有些人注定是为时代而生的，他们在某一个特定的时间点横空出世，影响并推动那个时代。容闳就是这样的人。"是的，时势造英雄亦英雄造时势。容闳，正是站在百年前的中国新旧交替的关口——皇朝与共和角力，文明与蒙昧竞争、黑暗与光明争夺的历史关节点，被时代选择为那个推动时代车轮前行的人物。他身上有众多"第一"的标签——史上第一位中国留美学生，引领中国走向世界的第一人，为中国现代工业奠基的第一人（中国第一个现代工厂——江南制造厂正是容闳一手参与采购西方机器并操办具体设立事务的），历史上第一次"公派留学生"的倡导者和执行人（容闳从耶鲁学成归国后，极力游说清廷，终获曾国藩之助而被李鸿章首肯，亲携"晚清留美学童"120人负笈美国，又以耶鲁为中心舞台，最后却因保守力量的干扰而被中途遣返挫败）；在我的认知中，容闳还是近现代中国在"西学东渐"的大环境下，挑头倡导"东学西渐"——重视中国文化的海外传播，推动西方图书馆典藏中国书籍的第一人。2019年耶鲁史特灵图书馆曾举办题为《"东学西渐"：耶鲁大学典藏东方书籍史迹》的大型展览，容闳为此作出的巨大贡献令世人瞩目。因之，无论从哪一个意义上说，容闳都是近现代中国史中一个无可忽略也无可替代、留下过深刻足迹的历史巨人。

然而，在媒体发达、信息畅通的当今舆论场域，容闳其人、其名、其声，却是常常被遮掩忽视而不为世人所识所知的。以我个人的具体经验，每当有远道而来的中国客人造访耶鲁而我需要担当导游角色的场合，我总喜欢把参观史特灵纪念图书馆的客人们带到展厅里展示的容闳铜像面前，却又每每听到这样的惊问："容闳"是谁？当他们听说完我详细的介绍讲述后，也同样会惊诧：为什么这么有分量的一位历史人物，我们这些受过高等教育的人，更别说一般中国人，却都全然不知晓？！——正是在这样一种貌似繁茂却每多荒芜的舆情现状中，这本图文并茂的《容闳图传》的出版，可谓是适得其所又适当其时也！翻开书页，一帧帧极其珍贵、既富带历史陈迹又散发着岁月幽香的图片和文字，将晚清迄今近两百年的相关史实立体可信、有触有感地呈现在读者面前。如同西哲所言："一切历史都是当代史"。此书充实丰盈的容闳史迹，对当代与后世的启迪——包括历史先贤的史迹求索与辉光照映，史观史识的当代观照与传承，"长河后浪"站在巨人肩头追赶"先辈前浪"的簇新创造等等——也就是常言道的"继往开来、存亡继绝"的意义吧，真是怎么珍视都难拎其重、怎么高看都全不为过的。我特别为"岁口"尚如此年轻的作者，在此书纷繁的史料考据、图片搜集与甄别等等所花费的巨大心力、所呈现出来的超凡功力感到由衷的钦敬和欣慰！

末了，把我曾为耶鲁先贤容闳及其名著《西学东渐记》写下的一首七言律句录于下，作为本文的收篇吧——

"掀篇蓦见旧风神，鴂语乡音带土亲。投枕惟追博海梦，守书犹见照灯痕。巉然湘棘存知己，幸也粤风有继人。愧欠先生三万里，迷津待渡尚初辰！"

（小注：鴂（音"决"）语，难懂的语言，此处指洋文；"湘棘"指游说曾国藩获支持的"晚清留美学童"事件；"三万里"，常言"去国万里"，容闳为许国而三度去国，最后于1912年病逝美国康州。）

2023年11月12日晨于耶鲁

（本文作者系中国旅美作家、著名学者，任教于耶鲁大学东亚语言系）

My Grandfather Yung Wing

Yung Yungcheng Frank

In my early years I had very little knowledge of who my grandfather Yung Wing was. My father passed away 10 days after I came into this world. My mother told me as a young boy that my grandfather was the first Chinese graduate in an American university. To a child it was akin to the first man to climb a mountain.

That state of consciousness continued until my early teens. I should add my Uncle Bartlett's family were always full of love and kindness to me as a child but I was perhaps too young to benefit from such a serious subject as Yung Wing's history. However, around the time when I was in my early teens several scholars and authors sought me out, and they sent me literature about Yung Wing. I also found a copy of *My Life in China and America*. So began a state of slow and gradual awakening to the life of my grandfather.

It would be natural for me to be grateful to the many authors and academics who initiated my interests in Yung Wing. Indeed, this feeling exists to this very day. I strongly appreciate the interests of modern-day academics in Yung Wing. I am also grateful to my friend Xu Hui Ping who is undertaking a biography of my grandfather. I know her intention for her book to be an inspiration to young men and women to step up to serve their nation, as Yung Wing had done one and a half century ago. I know her to be someone of talent and hard work, and wish her success.

In this article I shall go light on history but refer to sentiments, perhaps as grandson I am privileged to do. To start off, I would speculate who were the people for whom YW would have most gratitude in his later years.

In chronologic order, chief among his benefactors would be the Rev. Samuel Brown, without whom the journey to New England would not have started; the Ladies Association of Savannah who provided the major financial support for university education; viceroy Tsang Kwoh Fan who laid the ground work for court approval of CEM, and the Rev. Joseph Twichell, his lifelong friend who encouraged his marriage to Mary Kellogg and later help bring up my dad Morrison and my Uncle Bartlett.

Of course, without doubt he would also remember the kindness of the many others in Hong Kong and New York, who helped with financial assistance; his friends who introduced him to Tsang Kwoh Fan, including Governor Ting Yih Chang who played a role in gaining court approval for CEM. Then in addition to how my grandfather would feel towards the Rev. Twichell. If I may add a small addendum. I had occasion to sit in the pew at the Reverend's Asylum Hill Church in 1998, when in humble recognition of family history, I thanked the Lord for the marriage of my grandparents. This was the church where the Rev Twichell performed the ceremony and I cannot imagine any more appropriate place for me to pray in gratitude.

History tells us YW worked for 17 years to achieve his dream, to enable as many of his countrymen to be given the opportunity to have an education that he had. However not as much is told of what a fortunate turn of events led to the actual composition of his 120 young boys. Look at it this way, YW was over the moon when the approving imperial order for CEM came through. Before he organised the logistics and training preparations for the young boys, it was recognised that the recruitment of the youngsters would be an unforeseen major hurdle. It must have been a big question, which parents were prepared to allow their teenage sons to travel a long journey to a distant land to be educated by unfamiliar foreigners. As far as I know the recruitment strategy has not been mentioned in any detail, however the resultant numbers indicate the low hanging fruit approach. Of the young boys, 24 were from his native Zhuhai area, another 59 from his provincial Guangdong. (These numbers include 4 nephews and relatives with surname Yung) and the balance 26 from the China's coastal provinces.

I have little doubt that all the young boys were of fair intelligence, I dare to add many of them were highly talented teens. From stories of the 120, so many were outstanding in language, sports and social skills. They went on to academic achievements with relative ease, overcoming the hurdle of being in foreign land and learning a new language. They were well positioned to be inspired by YW's patriotism, spirit of reform and single mindedness as a pioneer. When they returned to China a good number became significant contributors to their nation. I will not repeat here the names nor their stories as these are told in many historical books. However, I would like to make the point that as YW has been acknowledged as the father of overseas education and for the CEM's overall acclaim, a fair portion of credit could be attributed to the achievements of the 120 young boys. History should be grateful that the 120 young boys carried the CEM torch with dignity and honour. Many of the 120 had distinguished and senior careers in government, universities, railway, and armed forces. It should also be borne in mind that the 120 had to overcome extraordinary difficulties as China was then ruled by a Ching court not in favour of innovation and ignorant of finance and market forces.

If I may I would digress and relate a story concerning the 120. From the time in 1872 when they arrived in America, YW placed them with selected local families in Connecticut and Massachusetts, the two states where the schools were situated. It was not only for the boys to learn English naturally but they would absorb local culture for their benefit. I would add that the character and upbringing of the young boys were such that, they had excellent relationship with their host families. There were many accounts of long-standing friendships. Now in America at this time there was a frenzy of anti-Chinese sentiment arising from labour sources which was concerned with loss of employment. This feeling reached a high pitch in US congress and resulted in the Chinese Exclusion Act in 1882. I need not go into detail of the discriminatory laws but I will say that when the Act was debated in congress, two states, Connecticut and Massachusetts voted against it. This account was told me by a gentleman I met at the Connecticut Historical Society. Imagine in the short space of only a few years, the behaviour of the 120 who represented a minute section of the Chinese nation were able to create such good impression and influenced the legislators of the states where they resided to oppose that discriminatory law. It makes me very proud of the 120 young boys. YW would have been very proud of them too.

I should not end my story without also mentioning the descendants of the 120 many of whom also served their country well. I will refer to one particular feature of the descendants. In 1998 Richard Yung, grandson of Yung Hoy and a cousin of mine, organised the first descendants' reunion at Yale University. And Yale was gracious to provide facilities for the gathering of only 4 descendants families (D-CEM). Subsequently there were one more such reunion at Yale and 3 more in Zhuhai over a period of some 15 years. This indicates how the D-CEM regard their grand-fathers lives, let me explain why the descendants are special to me.

I dare say all of these descendants grew up to become proud of their forebears, for their deeds that inspired young men and women. In my case I have made a fair number of lifelong friends who are in the grand-children generation of the 120. On first contact with them, I could sense a close relationship waiting to blossom. Some of them would say to me "…without your grandfather, we would not be where we are today." My very natural response would be "without Rev. Brown, none of us would be where we are today…" I have spent many enjoyable times exchanging family stories and of our careers with the CEM descendants. I consider these friendship a gift from heaven. I am indeed very grateful for the associations and mutual respect with my 120 family!

Several schools are named after YW and his statue stands in universities in Guangtung as well as Yale. There are libraries and museums to commemorate his name. There has been for some years in Zhuhai a research Institute dedicated to careers of YW and his young boys. The value YW leaves behind is a good example for younsters not only of China but for all nations to follow.

5 /11/ 2023 Singapore.

我的祖父容闳

容永成

　　我年幼的时候，对祖父容闳知之甚少。因为我出生仅十天，父亲容觐彤（Morrison Brown Yung）便去世了。母亲告诉我，我的祖父是第一位从美国大学毕业的中国人。对于一个孩子来说，这就像第一个攀登山峰的人。这种意识状态贯穿了我的少年时光。值得一提的是，叔叔容觐槐（Bartlett Golden Yung）的家庭总是充满着爱意和仁慈。可能是我太年幼，还无法从像容闳这样的严肃主题中受益。然而，在我十几岁的时候，几位学者和作家找到了我，并且寄给我有关容闳的文献。我也找到了一本《西学东渐记》（My life in China and America）的副本。就这样，我开始慢慢被唤醒，去了解祖父的生活。

　　对于那些激发我对容闳的兴趣的学者和作家，我至今心存感激。感谢当代学者对容闳的关注。我的朋友徐惠萍正在撰写一本关于我祖父的传记，目的是要激励年轻一代像150年前的容闳一样报效祖国，对此我非常感谢。她是一个才华横溢且勤勉敬业的人，祝她成功。

　　对于留学史实，毋庸我详细描述，但是作为容闳的嫡孙，我对留学史有着浓厚的感情。我首先推测容闳晚年会最感激哪些人：按时间顺序，首先容闳最应该感激的人应该是布朗牧师（Rev. Samuel Robbins Brown），如果没有他，容闳的留美之行就不会开始；其次是萨伐那妇女协会（Ladies Association of Savannah）为他的大学教育提供了主要的经济支持，曾国藩总督为留美幼童计划获朝廷恩准奠定了重要的基础；以及他的终身朋友吐依曲尔牧师（Rev. Joseph Hopkins Twichell）鼓励他与玛丽（Mary Louisa Kellogg）结婚，并帮助抚养我的父亲容觐彤和我的叔叔容觐槐；毫无疑问，他也会记得其他的一些在香港和纽约的好心人，以及介绍他结识曾国藩的朋友，包括一直助推留美幼童（Chinese Education Mission）计划的丁日昌。除了祖父对吐依曲尔牧师的感激之外，我还补充一点自己的感受。1998年，我拜访了吐依曲尔牧师工作过的避难山教堂（Asylum Hill Church），有幸坐在教堂长椅上，谦卑地认识家族的历史，感谢上帝赐予我祖父母婚姻。这里是吐依曲尔牧师为我祖父母主持婚礼的教堂，没有什么地方比这更适合我祈祷，以表达感恩之情了。

众所周知，容闳为实现留美幼童计划，使尽可能多的中国人有机会接受他所受过的教育，持之以恒17年之久。然而，一个幸运的事件是如何成就了他的120个留美幼童的梦想，却没有多少记载。当留美幼童计划被皇帝批准时，容闳欣喜若狂。在他为留美幼童组织后勤和培训准备之前，就已经意识到招生将成为一个不可忽略的主要障碍。那时候的父母怎么会同意把十几岁的孩子送往遥远的陌生之地接受洋人的教育呢。据我所知，招生策略虽然没有被详细地提及，但是招生结果的数字内涵却完全出乎意料。这些留美幼童之中，24人直接来自他的家乡珠海，另外60人来自广东省其他地方（其中包括4个姓容的侄子和亲戚），其余36人来自中国其他省份。

我毫不怀疑留美幼童的聪明才智，他们中许多人都是极有才华的青少年。从这120人的故事来看，他们中的许多人在语言、运动和社交技能方面都非常出色，相对轻松地取得了学业成就，克服了在异国他乡学习新语言的障碍；容闳的爱国主义、改革精神和作为先驱者的一心一意激励了他们。当他们回到中国时，许多人成为国家的重要贡献者。无须在这里重复他们的姓名和故事，因为这些都在许多历史书籍中有记载。然而，需要指出的是，容闳被誉为"中国留学生之父"，以及留美幼童获得的整体好评，一定程度上功劳归于这120人的成就。历史应该感激这120人以尊严和荣誉的方式传递了留美幼童计划的火炬。这120个人之中，有许多人在政府、大学、铁路和军队中担任高级职务，由于中国当时还是由一个不支持创新、对金融和市场力量一无所知的清廷所统治，所以这120个人必须克服非凡的困难。

再讲述一个与120名留美幼童相关的故事。从1872年他们到达美国开始，容闳就把他们安置在康涅狄格州和马萨诸塞州的当地家庭——这些家庭都是精心挑选的，这不仅有利于留美幼童自然熟悉英语，而且有利于他们吸收当地文化。我要补充的是，这些留美幼童的性格和教养使得他们与寄宿家庭保持了良好的关系，有的友谊甚至持续了很多年。此时的美国，由于担心失业，劳工中出现了一股反华情绪。这种情绪在美国国会中达到了高潮，并导致了1882年的《排华法案》。我不需要详细说明歧视性的法律，但我要说的是，当该法案在美国国会辩论时，康涅狄格州和马萨诸塞州投了反对票。这个故事是我从康涅狄格州历史学会认识一位先生那里听到的。试想一下，在短短几年的工夫，这些仅仅代表中华民族极小部分的120人的行为，竟然能够留下如此良好的印象，并且影响了他们所在州的立法者反对歧视性法律。这120个留美幼童，让我感到非常骄傲。容闳也一定会为他们感到骄傲的。

最后不能不提的是，这120名留美幼童的后代，他们中的许多人也为国家做出了贡献。我认为这是留美幼童后代的一个共同特点。1998年，容星桥的孙子，也是我的表亲容应骞（Richard Yung），在耶鲁大学组织了第一次留美幼童后代聚会。虽然只有4个留美幼童后代家庭，但是耶鲁大学还是很慷慨地提供了聚会场地。此后的15年时间里，这样的聚会在耶鲁大学至少举行了一次，在珠海也至少举行了三次，这说明了留美幼童后代对他们祖父辈的敬仰。我想解释一下，为什么作为留美幼童后代会很特别。我敢说，由于留美幼童的事迹激励了青年男女，所有留美幼童的后代长大后，都会为他们的祖先感到自豪。就我而言，我和相当多的留美幼童后代成为终身朋友。在初次与他们接触时，我就能感受到彼此之间似乎有一种与生俱来的亲密关系。他们中的一些人会对我说："……没有你的祖父，我们今天就不会在这里。"我很自然地回答道："没有布朗牧师，我们谁也不会在这里。"我和留美幼童后代们分享了许多家族故事和我们的职业生涯。这些友谊对我来说，是上天赐予的礼物。对于120个留美幼童家族建立的联系和相互尊重，我深表感激！

现在有几所以容闳命名的学校，他的雕像也矗立在广东和耶鲁大学的校园中，许多图书馆和博物馆也在纪念他，珠海还有多年研究容闳与留美幼童的协会。容闳留下的价值，不仅是中国年轻一代最好的榜样，而且也是所有国家的年轻人效仿的榜样。

2023年11月5日于新加坡

（本文作者系容闳嫡孙，新加坡电信局原主席）

第一章　南屏少年

(1828—1846)

The Youth from Nanping

（1）1828年/容闳出生

清道光八年，戊子年十一月十七日，容闳出生于广东省香山县南屏乡（今珠海市南屏镇）的一个普通农家。父亲容丙炎，母亲林莲娣。据《香山县志续编》记载，容闳始祖为南汉时期陇西敦煌沙祖公，宋末沙祖公九世孙六二祖公迁徙至时称沙尾村的南屏乡，开枝散叶，成为南屏第一大姓。香山县是广东古县，主要包括今天的澳门、珠海、中山的大部分地区。"一八二八年十一月十七日，予生于彼多罗岛之南屏镇。镇距澳门西南约四英里。澳门，葡萄牙殖民地也。岛与澳门间，有海峡广半英里许。予第三，有一兄一姊一弟。今兄弟若姊俱已谢世，惟予仅存。"（摘自容闳自传《西学东渐记》，以下简称《西学东渐记》）。

是年，和容闳一起留学美国的黄宽，在珠海东岸村出生。

1828/Yung Wing was born.

On November 17, Yung Wing was born to an ordinary farming family in Nanping Township (now Nanping Town, Zhuhai) in Xiangshan County, Guangdong Province. His father was Rong Bingyan, and his mother was Lin Liandi. According to the *Continuation of the Xiangshan County Annals*, Yung Wing's ancestor moved to Nanping Township during the Song Dynasty and became the most common surname in Nanping.

○ 图1-1 容闳故居（今珠海
南屏镇南屏社区西大街3巷1
号）和容闳使用过的水井

口二百六十餘人

潭石馮族始祖肎周由順德牛頭山馬江鄉開四房次房仲魁遷居東莞海南柵鄉後遷香山城東門復遷南界涌六世祖恆簡始遷潭井現歷十九代丁口七十餘人

下恭鎮

南屏容族始祖六二宋嘉定間自新會遷來六二生光祖光祖生八子遂分八房由光祖至今歷二十二代丁口一千有奇

南屏林族始祖勝和明洪武十九年自黃梁都泥灣村遷來分五房現歷十九代丁口五十餘人

南屏張族分二支其一支始祖萬八宋咸淳四年自南雄珠璣巷遷來後分二房現歷二十四代丁口五百餘人 又一

○ 图1-2　上图为《香山县志续编》关于南屏容族的记载。下图为容闳父母墓碑，位于今珠海市南屏镇黑面将军山的橘树山上

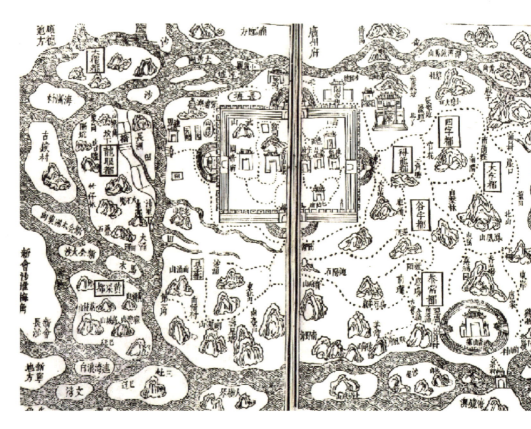

o 图1-3 1750年的香山县地图。香山县建于南宋1152年，县址设在濠潭（今珠海山场村），后迁中山石岐。地图右下角放大图上，沙尾就是容闳的出生地，所在岛屿即容闳回忆录中的彼多罗岛，与小岛隔水相望的濠镜澳即澳门，图中心高墙环抱的香山寨即闻名遐迩的军事要塞前山寨

1829年/容闳1岁

　　伴随着大航海时代的开启和欧洲殖民主义者的扩张，1553年，葡萄牙人租住澳门，连通世界的新航路延伸至此，澳门成为中国第一通商口岸和西方人在华的第一个合法居住地，容闳的家乡也因缘际会成为华夏大地最早感受西方文明的近水楼台。1574年，明朝在澳门和今珠海相连处莲花茎设官驻守，建立了中国最早的关闸，史称"茎半设闸"。1688年，清朝在澳门设立海关机构——粤海关澳门总口，下辖四个关口，新航线上的东方大港日益繁荣兴盛。伏在亲人臂弯里的容闳，耳边不时响起远洋商船的汽笛声和河对岸澳门西洋教堂的钟声。

1829/Yung Wing was 1 year old.

　　Xiangshan County is an ancient county mainly covering most of today's Macao, Zhuhai, and Zhongshan. In 1553, the Portuguese obtained the right to lease Macao, making it the first legal place of residence for Westerners in China and the first commercial port connecting Chinese society to the Western world.

关闸口

大码头口

澳门总口

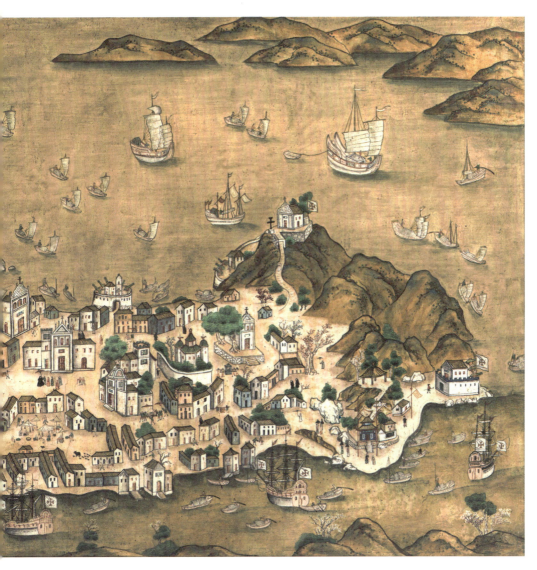

o 图1-4　18世纪澳门全图。这是目前发现最早完整可见澳门总口及其下辖四关口工作场景图，依稀可见身着顶戴花翎的海关人员。原图为澳门圣若瑟修院壁画

o 图1-5　图为欧洲人开辟的新航路延伸到澳门
【审图号：粤CS（Z022）013号】

o 图1-6　1598年的拜耶亚马港（澳门）
城图。这是最早一张由西方版画家绘制
的澳门铜版画地图，描绘了澳门开埠初
期的面貌

o 图1-7　澳门和珠海水陆相连，陆地以一条沙堤连
接，称为莲花茎，建有关闸楼，早期关闸楼楼高三
层，门楣刻有"关闸门"，后多次修建。图为1844
年《伦敦新闻画报》中的澳门关闸远眺图

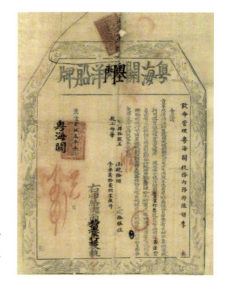

o 图1-8　"广东诸泊口，最是澳门雄"。所有外国商船必
须在粤海关澳门总口纳税、申办进港船牌、聘请引水员和通
事等。图为1758年粤海关澳门总口颁发给外国商船的船牌

（2）1830年/容闳2岁

　　澳门开埠后，这里成为西方传教士进入中国的第一站，他们在这里兴办西学，传播新知识新思想，利玛窦、汤若望、南怀仁、郎世宁等著名的传教士都是通过这里进入中国内地的，香山县也成为近代中国接触西方世界的最前沿窗口。从容闳家乡南屏的山上可以看到的澳门圣保禄教堂是当年远东最大的天主教堂，容闳七岁的时候，这座闻名遐迩的教堂付之一炬，所余前壁就是今天广为人知的大三巴牌坊。

1830/Yung Wing was 2 years old.

　　Macao was established as the first stop for Western missionaries entering China. Famous missionaries such as Matteo Ricci, Johann Adam Schall von Bell, Giulio Aleni, and Lodovico Buglio entered the Chinese mainland through Macao. The St. Paul's Church in Macao, which could be seen from Yung Wing's hometown, was the largest Catholic church in the Far East at that time.

○ 图1-9 左图取自《香山县志》，展示了从容闳家乡远眺澳门半岛西面的场景。左下角的前山与容闳出生的南屏都在彼多罗岛，也称将军山岛。右图为在澳门穿着中国服装的外国传教士

○ 图1-10 图为烧毁前后的澳门圣保禄教堂

（3）1831年/容闳3岁

在距离容闳家乡100多公里的广州，英国东印度公司举办了第4届洋人们的划船比赛，这是中国境内最早的西式船赛。1757年，随着清政府关闭沿海关口，仅保留粤海关"一口通商"，广州口岸及其外港澳门，成为当时闭关锁国下唯一幸存的对外交往通道，独揽中国外贸长达85年。香山县也在一口通商的大环境下，占尽天时地利，成为近代中国接触西方世界的最前沿窗口。"洋船争出是官商，十字门开向二洋，五丝八丝广缎好，银钱堆满十三行"，明末清初广东诗人屈大均的这首竹枝词，描绘出从广州口岸到容闳家乡十字门水域繁忙的商贸景象。

是年，知名书画家、香山县山场村（今珠海山场社区）时任刑部主事的鲍俊辞官还乡，后来创建了石溪摩崖石刻群，即今天的石溪公园。

1831/Yung Wing was 3 years old.

In Guangzhou, more than 100 kilometers from Rong Hong's hometown, the British East India Company held the 4th boating competition for foreigners. This was the earliest Western-style boat race in China. Guangzhou had become the main area for China's foreign trade. In 1757, China had closed its ports to trade, except Guangzhou and Macao.

○ 图1-11　广州十三行是清廷1684年成立的对外贸易垄断机构，各国商馆林立，繁华熙攘

○ 图1-12 按照当时规定，广州贸易季节结束，外国商人需返回本国或移住澳门，称为"下澳住冬"，形成"贸易地-广州，居住地-澳门"格局，图为澳门南湾的洋房

o 图1-13　随着澳门成为新航线上的东方枢纽港，容闳家乡十字门水域商船云集。图为停泊在此的各国船只

（4）1832年/容闳4岁

　　容闳家乡与澳门水陆相连，鸡犬之声相闻，得风气之先的父老乡亲习惯于到澳门打工，做小生意，赚洋人的钱。"岭外云深抹翠微，翠微村外落花飞，负贩纷纷多估客，辛苦言从澳里来。" 1684年，两广总督吴兴祚陪同钦差大臣石柱视察澳门时作的诗歌，描绘了容闳家乡的翠微村民（今珠海翠微村）来往澳门做生意的繁忙情景。

　　是年，基督新教最早的中文布道书——《劝世良言》在广州问世，编著者梁发是中国第一个华人基督教牧师。"马礼逊有一最著名之事业，曾于中国得第一耶教信徒，名梁亚发。其人能本耶教宗旨，著成传道书数种。洪秀全求道时，即以马氏所译圣经，及梁氏所著书，通习研究。"（摘自《西学东渐记》）

　　是年，5月19日，容闳同窗好友、中国近代民族企业家先驱唐廷枢，在今珠海唐家湾出生。

1832 / Yung Wing was 4 years old.

　　Yung Wing lived in a town which was connected to Macao by water and land. The local elders were accustomed to working in Macao, operating small businesses and earning money from foreigners.

○ 图1-14 澳门南湾街头的华人渔夫和轿夫

○ 图1-15 图为澳门玫瑰堂前的华人小摊贩和奔波在水面上摇着舢板的华人妇女

（5）1833年/容闳5岁

　　越来越多的外国鸦片走私船涌入容闳家乡淇澳岛附近的伶仃、金星门海域，这里成为新的鸦片集散中心，当年交货的鸦片高达2万多箱。10月15日，外国鸦片船队武装袭击今珠海淇澳岛，容闳的父老乡亲们誓死抵抗，用土枪土炮击退了洋人，迫使洋人赔款白银三千两，村民用此赔款铺筑了两公里长的花岗岩路，即今天的白石街。这是晚清中国第一次，也是唯一的一次获得西方列强赔款。"十三年春，有夷船来泊金星门，踵至者五十余只。淇澳乡人白上官，驱之，乃去。"（摘自《香山县志》）孩子们开始传唱这样的民谣："道光十三年，番鬼入村庄，打死人和畜，抢走牛和粮。"

1833/Yung Wing was 5 years old

　　Yung Wing's hometown near Qiao Island was filled with an increasing number of foreign opium smuggling ships. On October 15th, a fleet of foreign opium ships attacked Qiao Island. Yung Wing's fellow villagers vowed to resist to the death and forced the foreigners to surrender and pay 3,000 taels of silver as compensation. They used these funds to build a two-kilometer-long granite road, now known as Baishi Street.

○ 图1-16　图为当时抗击侵略者的炮台

○ 图1-17　左图为淇澳岛天后宫和白石街碑刻，记载了当时的抗英斗争。右图为淇澳岛民众利用洋人赔款修筑的白石街

（6）1834年/容闳6岁

是年，普鲁士籍传教士郭士腊的英国妻子温斯蒂在澳门开设女校，这是西方传教士在中国开展女子教育的最初尝试。同年8月，进入中国的第一位基督新教传教士——马礼逊在广州去世。他来华传教25年，在译经书、编字典、办刊物、设学校和开医馆等方面都有首创之功。"马礼逊博士既在中国成如许事业，其名永垂不朽。"（摘自《西学东渐记》）

1834/Yung Wing was 6 years old

The English wife of Prussian missionary Karl Gutzlaff, known as Mrs. Gutzlaff, opened a girls' school in Macao, marking the first attempt by Western missionaries to provide education for Chinese girls. That same year, the first Protestant missionary to enter China, Robert Morrison, passed away in Guangzhou. Yung Wing writes that "Dr. Morrison's accomplishments in China will be forever remembered."（from *My Life in China and America*）.

o 图1-18　晚清传教士开设的女子教会学校

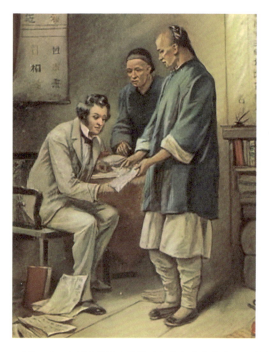

o 图1-19　左图为传教士马礼逊在华人教徒李十公、陈老宜协助下翻译圣经。右图为位于澳门基
督教坟场的马礼逊墓碑

（7）1835年/容闳7岁

是年，为纪念马礼逊，部分英美在华外交官、商人、传教士成立马礼逊教育协会，创办马礼逊预备学校，免费提供食宿，吸引贫寒子弟。预备学校附设在郭士腊夫人的女校。

9月，容闳随父亲到澳门，入读这所学校。"当时中国为纯粹之旧世界，仕进显达，赖八股为敲门砖，予兄入读私塾，独命予入读西校，此则百思不得其故。意者通商而后，所谓洋务渐趋重要，吾父母预先着人鞭，翼儿子能出人头地，得一翻译或洋务委员之优缺乎。至于后来所成之事业，似为时势所趋，非吾父母所料及也。"（摘自《西学东渐记》）

1835 / Yung Wing was 7 years old

In that year, to commemorate Dr. Morrison, some British and American diplomats, businessmen, and missionaries in China established the Morrison Education Society and founded the Morrison School, a preparatory school that was created and attached to Mrs. Gutzlaff's girl's school.

In September, Yung Wing enrolled in this school.

o 图1-20 郭士腊夫人的女校设在自己租住的寓所大三巴巷187号，紧靠大三巴旁，史称"澳门女塾"。图为大三巴

ART. V. *Proceedings relative to the formation of the Morrison Education Society ; including the Constitution, names of the Trustees and members, with remarks explanatory of the object, of the Institution.*

[The Trustees of this society, elected on the 9th ultimo, for the current year, are Lancelot, Dent esq., President; Thomas Fox, esq., Vice-president; William Jardine, esq., Treasurer; Rev. E. C. Bridgman, Corresponding Secretary ; and J. Robt. Morrison, esq., Recording Secretary. A pamphlet which they have just published (the title of which stands at the head of this article) we introduce here, somewhat abridged ; and we fondly hope that wherever the object of the Society is made known, it will receive the cordial approbation and support of the friends of China.

Nor long after the lamented death of the Rev. Robert Morrison, D.D., on the 1st of August 1834, a paper containing some suggestions for the formation of an association, to be called the MORRISON EDUCA-TION SOCIETY, was circulated among the foreign residents in China. This paper was dated the 26th January, 1835. On the 24th of the next month, twenty-two signatures having been obtained, and the sum of $4860 collected, a Provisional Committee—consisting of six

o 图1-21 容闳初见郭士腊夫人，对她的穿着打扮惊诧不已，尤其是两只隆起的袖子"圆博如球"。左图为当时澳门西方妇女穿着的流行裙装。右图为《中国丛报》关于马礼逊教育协会成立的相关报道，报道称当时有22人参与教育协会，募集到资金4860美元

（8）1836年/容闳8岁

澳门，预备学校一年级就读，跟着郭士腊夫人和她的侄女派克司姐妹二人，学习英文、科学课程，跟着中文老师学习四书五经等儒家经典书籍。第一次离家，容闳对陌生的环境有些不适应，组织六个同学乘船出逃被追回。"虽夫人和颜悦色，终揣揣也，我生之初，足迹不出里巷，骤易处境，自非童稚所堪。"（摘自《西学东渐记》）

1836/ Yung Wing was 8 years old

Yung Wing enrolled in the first grade of the preparatory school. He studied English and science with Mrs. Gutzlaff and Chinese with a Chinese teacher. He also studied the Confucian classics.

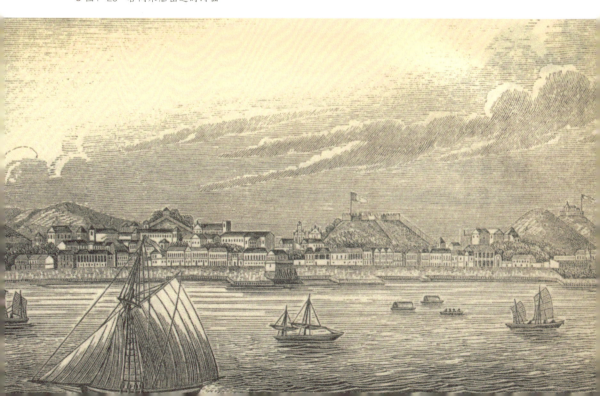

4　MY LIFE IN CHINA AND AMERICA

long and full flowing white dress (the interview took place in the summer), surrounded by two large globe sleeves which were fashionable at the time and which lent her an exaggerated appearance, I remember most vividly I was no less puzzled than stunned. I actually trembled all over with fear at her imposing proportions —having never in my life seen such a peculiar and odd fashion. I clung to my father in fear. Her kindly expression and sympathetic smiles found little appreciative response at the outset, as I stood half dazed at her personality and my new environment. For really, a new world had dawned on me. After a time, when my home-sickness was over and the novelty of my sur-roundings began gradually to wear away, she completely won me over through her kindness and sympathy. I began to look upon her more like a mother. She seemed to take a special interest in me; I suppose, because I was young and helpless, and away from my parents, besides being the youngest pupil in the school. She kept me among her girl pupils and did not allow me to mingle with what few boys there were at the time.

There is one escapade that I can never forget! It happened during the first year in

BOYHOOD　5

the school, and was an attempt on my part to run away. I was shut up in the third story of the house, which had a wide open terrace on the top,—the only place where the girls and myself played and found recreation. We were not allowed to go out of doors to play in the streets. The boy pupils had their quarters on the ground floor and had full liberty to go out for exercise. I used to envy them their freedom and smuggled down stairs to mingle with them in their sports after school hours. I felt ill at ease to be shut up with the girls all alone way up in the third story. I wanted to see something of the outside world. I occasionally stole down stairs and ventured out to the wharves around which were clustered a number of small ferry boats which had a peculiar fascination to my young fancy. To gain my freedom, I planned to run away. The girls were all much older than I was, and a few sympathized with me in my wild scheme; doubtless, from the same restlessness of being too closely cooped up. I told them of my plan. Six of the older ones fell in with me in the idea. I was to slip out of the house alone, go down to the wharf and engage a covered boat to take us all in.
The next morning after our morning meal,

予儿时嗜游泳，第一入塾时普通学，其事至今不忘。古夫人之居学于女塾，本为优遇，不知其同遇，予不知其何故。男生等曾居楼下阁，纲栏户外运动，而予与诸女伴，期循楼于三层楼上，惟以鼎台为游戏场，以为有所限禁，心不能甘，常谓余街市，与男生辈，又赴楼等营许自由出门，故步街市，而于等既无此权利，心益不平，乃时时潜往至码头，见小舟散集，意复荡漾，思取此而返出舟集，以复我自

由之日，同院女生，年事皆长于予，中有数人，因禁闭过严，亦久鹜居此，放于予之计划，探索同情，既得同志六人，胆益壮，定计予先至埠头，雇定盖船小船，乘闻取逐，悉晨曼同行，敝晨大书渡前，亦寄胜登舟，向知异道发，对界为彼多罗马，予家在也。遵同伴六人先至予幸小仕，然后分据五，于乃得圆自以为出万全，不暇江来半，追若溯下。未能就道，转瞬且昆。予乃恼急，促待予力前进，予覆发促坤时瞬以此金。但于为只二掉，即掉互有力，舟子知势力急乱，舟来舟手小一掉，即被舟集同，坐子圆子此舟，放誓入堂，乃施短成，古夫人聚合予等排用或行，速行全校。且于饮膳后，课堂中盘一长桌，合七人义其上一小时，于文中央，左右各三人，头藏尖圆圆桶，陶遗盖一方辞大书恭赴，不曾恬累摩四处，于受此恐辱，愈惧无地。坐于古夫人素缺未足，故将果樱楼子等分给他生调食，使予愉而躁痛，他不一顾，吾庆相顾，唯堪滋瓷，古夫人陶恶予测渍，

○ 图1-22　《西学东渐记》中关于容闳就读马礼逊预备学校期间乘船出逃的记载

○ 图1-23　容闳乘船出逃的河面

（9）1837年/容闳9岁

澳门，预备学校二年级就读。学校继续扩大，已有12名女生和包括容闳在内的2名男生，其中有3位盲女。容闳辅导教他们凸字识文法，两年之后，他们已经能够用凸文识字法诵习《圣经》《天路历程》。后来三人随郭士腊夫人出国留学，成为中国最早的女留学生。其中一位盲女毕业之后回到宁波盲校任教。

1837/Yung Wing was 9 years old

Yung Wing entered the second grade of the preparatory school. Among his classmates were three blind girls. Yung Wing taught braille to the three blind girls, and two years later, they were able to read and recite the Bible using this method. Later, the three blind girls went abroad to study with Mrs. Gutzlaff, becoming China's earliest female students to study overseas.

○ 图1-24 容闳辅导过的三位盲女同学玛丽（左）、艾格利斯（中）和杰西（右）

○ 图1-25 盲女们在学习《圣经》

（10）1838年/容闳10岁

澳门，预备学校三年级就读。

时任湖广总督林则徐上书朝廷呼吁禁烟："此祸不出，十年之后，不唯无可筹之饷，且无可用之兵。"林则徐被任命为钦差大臣，从广州开始严禁鸦片，大批英国烟商纷纷从广州潜往澳门，涌入澳门的欧洲人之多前所未有。

是年，容闳的同乡好友、上海开埠先驱之一徐润在今珠海北岭社区出生。

1838/Yung Wing was 10 years old

In the third grade of the preparatory school.

Lin Zexu was appointed as the imperial minister. Starting from Guangzhou, opium was banned, and a large number of British tobacco merchants escaped from Guangzhou to Macau. The influx of Europeans to Macau was unprecedented.

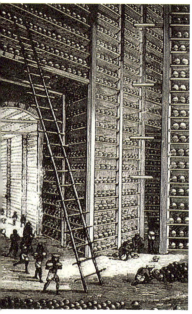

o 图1-26　左图为英国东印度公司的鸦片仓库。右图为漂浮在珠江口贩卖鸦片的英国趸船

o 图1-27　鸦片战争前夕的澳门护国庙前

（11）1839年/容闳11岁

澳门，预备学校四年级就读。

朝廷颁布禁烟令。6月，钦差大臣林则徐将收缴的两万多箱鸦片在虎门海滩当众销毁，史称"虎门销烟"。9月，林则徐在两广总督邓廷桢陪同下视察位于容闳家乡的海防要塞前山寨（今珠海前山），再次升格驻军将领，为抵御外敌做准备。随后，林则徐一行巡视容闳求学地澳门，所到之处，万人空巷。

战争一触即发，郭士腊夫人关闭学校回英国。容闳辍学回南屏老家。

是年11月，中国第一所西式学校——马礼逊学校在澳门正式开学，马礼逊教育协会聘请美国纽约聋哑学校教师塞缪尔·布朗担任校长。

1839/Yung Wing was 11 years old

In the fourth grade of the preparatory school. In June, the imperial envoy Lin Zexu publicly destroyed over 20,000 boxes of opium. This became known as the famous "Humen Opium Ban ".With war imminent, Mrs. Gutzlaff closed the preparatory school. Yung Wing dropped out of school and returned home.

At the end of the year, the Morrison School officially opened in Macao with the American educator Rev. Samuel Brown as the principal.

o 图1-28 钦差大臣林则徐和虎门销烟图

○ 图1-29　林则徐澳门巡视线路图

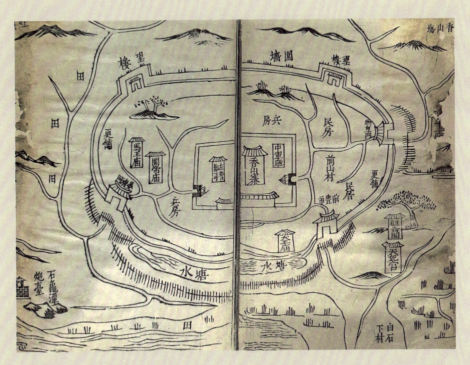

○ 图1-30　容闳家乡的前山寨是1621年朝廷为加强对澳门的管控而设立的军事要塞，这张《香山县志》1673年的前山寨图是迄今能够看到的最早记载

o 图1-31　上图为抗英名将关天培将军使用的前山寨澳门军事地图，下图为林则徐在前山寨写下的十无益格言原碑拓片

（12）1840年/容闳12岁

辍学返乡又遭遇父亲病故，与哥哥姐姐一起分担家庭重担，走村串寨兜售糖果，下田收割稻子，到澳门印刷厂折叠书页，赚取微薄银子贴补家用。"予父逝世，身后萧条，家无担石，予兄弟姐妹四人，三人年纪稍长，能博微资，予兄业渔，予姐操持家务，予亦往来于本乡及邻镇之间贩卖糖果，兢兢业业，不敢视为儿戏，每日清晨三时即起，到晚上六时始归，日获银币二角五分，悉以奉母。"（摘自《西学东渐记》）

8月，在距离容闳家乡南屏七里地的地方，英军突袭关闸，前山寨官兵奋起反击，终不抵敌，这是鸦片战争的第一次军事冲突，史称"中英关闸之战"。

11月，命运出现转机。在澳门行医的英国传教士合信受郭士腊夫人委托，辗转找到容闳，送容闳重新入读马礼逊学校，完成郭士腊夫人心愿。

1840/Yung Wing was 12 years old.

After dropping out of school and returning home, Yung Wing's father passed away. He and his siblings were now forced to share the burden of supporting the family. He roamed from village to village selling candy, harvesting rice in the fields, and folding book pages in Macao. In November, British missionary Dr. Ben jamin Hobson found Yung Wing. Mrs.Gutzlaff had entrusted Dr. Hobson to find Yung Wing and to encourage him to continue his studies at Morrison School.

o 图1-32 珠江三角洲稻田收割图，容闳辍学回乡后曾经下田收割稻谷

o 图1-33 左图为鸦片战争第一次军事冲突地澳门关闸。右图为受郭士腊夫人委托找到容闳的英国传教士合信

（13）1841年/容闳13岁

　　年初，入读澳门马礼逊学校。班上已有5名学生，其中4人来自今珠海地区，他们是唐廷桂、唐廷枢、黄宽和黄胜。马礼逊学校课程设置有别于传统私塾，这里有中国教师传授四书五经，有外国教师讲授数学、力学、生理学、西方历史、世界地理等西式课程。这些外国教师都是大学毕业的传教士，博学多才。这所以传播宗教为初衷的西式学校，客观上为近代中国培养了第一批率先接受西方科技文化的有用之才，比邻澳门的香山人近水楼台先得月，成为马礼逊学校的主要学生群体。

　　同年1月26日，英国派兵强行占领香港。

1841/Yung Wing was 13 years old.

　　At the beginning of the year, Yung Wing enrolled in Morrison School. This was China's first Western-style school. Although it was established to spread Christianity, it also nurtured China's first group of Western educated students. The people of Xiangshan, who lived close to Macao, became the main student group at Morrison School.

○ 图1-34 图为马礼逊学校首任校长、毕业于耶鲁大学的美国教育家塞缪尔·布朗

序号	英文名	中文名	年龄	籍贯	入学时间	备注
1	Aling	亚灵	16	澳门 Macao	1839年11月4日	
2	Ats'éuk	亚爵	14	山场 Shángchéung	1839年11月4日	
3	Ahóp	亚合	12	前山 Tsínshán	1839年11月4日	
4	Ayûn	亚远	11	山场Shángchéung	1839年11月4日	
5	Awai	亚伟	11	山场Shángchéung	1839年11月4日	
6	Achik	亚植	11	唐家 T'óngká	1839年11月4日	即唐廷桂
7	Akan	亚根	14	牛坑里 Ngauháng lai	1840年3月1日	即李根
8	Awan	亚运	11	澳门 Macao	1840年3月1日	即周运
9	Afún	亚宽	13	东岸 Tungngón	1840年3月13日	即黄宽
10	Alun	亚伦	10	澳门 Macao	1840年3月16日	
11	T'inyau	天佑	9	南屏 Námping	1840年3月28日	
12	Awing	亚闳	13	南屏 Námping	1840年11月1日	即容闳
13	Ashing	亚胜	15	澳门Macao	1841年11月1日	即黄胜
14	Akû	亚驱	10	唐家 T'óngká	1841年11月1日	即唐廷枢
15	Ats'au	亚秋	12	唐家 T'óngká	1841年11月1日	
16	Ayuk	亚沃	11	唐家 T'óngká	1841年11月1日	
17	Ayûn	亚元	11	山头园 Shánt'au ûn	1841年11月1日	
18	Alik	亚力	11	官塘 Kúnt'óng	1841年11月1日	
19	Ami	亚未	12	南屏 Námping	1841年11月1日	
20	Akwái	亚携	11	崖口 Ngái hau	1841年11月1日	
21	Atsám	亚智	11	山头园 Shánt'au ûn	1841年11月1日	
22	Apó	亚宝	9	白石下 P'átsz' shek	1841年11月1日	
23	Atsó	亚坐	10	上栅 Shéungtsák	1841年11月1日	
24	Ahung	亚洪	11	上栅Shéungtsák	1841年11月1日	
25	Afûnlan	亚宽林	11	后坑 Hauháng	1841年11月1日	
26	Alam	亚林	11	下微（尾）Hámi	1841年11月1日	
27	Afai	亚辉	9	古鹤 Kúhók	1841年11月1日	
28	Aching	亚澄	9	古鹤 Kúhók	1841年11月1日	
29	Alammuk	亚林茂	10	白石下 P'átsz' shek	1841年11月1日	
30	Ashing	亚圣	9	宁波 Ningpo	1841年11月1日	
31	Ahing	亚庆	9	深州 Sámchau	1843年4月7日	
32	Afai	亚辉	9	黄埔 Whampoa	1843年4月7日	
33	Ashin	亚善	13	黄埔 Whampoa	1843年4月7日	
34	Shínsz'	善士	10	南京 Nanking	1843年4月7日	
35	Aiú	亚尧	12	唐家 T'óngká	1843年4月7日	
36	Alín	亚连	11	新村 Sántsûn	1843年4月7日	
37	Akwong	亚光	9	黄埔 Whampoa	1843年4月7日	
38	Láisz'	来士	9	南京 Nanking	1843年4月7日	
39	Ayamyau	亚壬酉	9	澳门 Macao	1843年4月7日	
40	Afú	亚扶	8	唐家 T'óngká	1843年4月7日	
41	Kwongchú	光珠	9	定海（Tinghái）	1843年5月15日	
42	T'ingsau	天秀	18	新加坡（Singapore）	1843年9月1日	

马礼逊学生总表（1839-1843）

马礼逊学校课程情况表

科目	课程详情	备注
数学	科尔伯恩（Colburn）《算术入门》《算术》《代数》和《心算》，高登（Gordon）的《算术》，普莱菲尔（Playfair）《几何学》，欧氏里得的《几何原本》等	
地理	帕利《儿童地理》（Peter Parley's Method of Telling about Geography to Children）、盖伊《学校地理课》（Joseph Guy's school geography）、摩里《学校地图集》（Sidney Edwards Morse's School Atlas）和《地理和地图》（Geography and Maps）、奥尼尔《地理入门》（Jesse Olney's Introduction to Geography）等	
历史	帕利《儿童版世界历史故事》（Peter Parley's Method of telling stories about the world to children）、休谟《英国历史》（David Hume's History）、凯特利《英国史教材》（Thomas Keightley's School History of England）等	
读写	盖劳特（Thomas Hopkins Gallaudet）的《拼根际蒙书——教孩子如何阅读》、《想学拼写教材》（Union Spelling Books）《学生大纲》（Intellectual Reader）、宾特《读者图解》（Rensselaer Bentley's Pictorial Reader）、古德里奇《第二读者》《第三读者》和《第三读者》（Goodrich's Second Reader, Goodrich's Third Reader）等	
宗教	《新约》、《旧约》、启勒的《福音书》等	
理学	牛顿的三大运动定律和其万有引力定律	
卫生	盖劳特《儿童心灵读本》（The Child's Book on the Soul）、泰勒女士（Mrs. Jane Taylor）《儿童生理》（Physiology for Children）、皮特（Harvey Prindle Peet）《聋哑人入门教材》（The First Course of Instruction for the Deaf and Dumb）等	
中文	《孔子》《孟子》《左传》《诗经》《易经》《诗经》等字典类，朱熹的《四书集注》，以及中文版《圣经》	

○ 图1-35 右上图为马礼逊学校学生表，标记粉红者出生村落位于今珠海。右下图为马礼逊学校课程表

（14）1842年/容闳14岁

　　入读马礼逊学校二年级，中英文水平得到很大提升，可以背诵中国古文经典，翻译中文版《新约》，背诵休谟《英国历史》节选。

　　8月29日，中英签订我国近代史上第一个不平等条约《南京条约》，香港岛被迫割让给英国，中国从此沦为半殖民地半封建社会。11月1日，马礼逊学校迁往香港维多利亚港摩利臣山，又称为飞鹅山书院，容闳随之前往继续学习。

　　是年，中国第一部介绍西方国家科学技术和世界地理历史知识的综合性图书《海国图志》刊行面世，首次提出"师夷长技以制夷"。这是魏源在林则徐《四洲志》基础上编纂的。

1842/Yung Wing was 14 years old

　　On August 29, the Qing court signed the first unequal treaty in modern Chinese history with the British government—called the "Treaty of Nanjing" .This treaty forced the cession of Hong Kong Island to Britain. In November of the same year, Morrison School moved to Mount Davis along the banks of Victoria Harbor in Hong Kong, and Yung Wing moved there to continue his studies.

o 图1-36 摩利臣山冈上的马礼逊学校及其细节图

o 图1-37 《南京条约》签署现场

（15）1843年/容闳15岁

就读香港马礼逊学校三年级。学习凯特利《英国史》、科尔伯恩《算术知识》以及英文写作和书法，英语语言能力稳步提高。

4月5日，24岁的英国维多利亚女王签署了《香港宪章》，正式宣布香港成为英国殖民地，设立香港总督职位。

是年，容闳马礼逊学校同乡好友唐廷桂作为英国首任驻上海领事巴富尔翻译前往上海，成为最早参与上海开埠的香山人之一。

1843/Yung Wing was 15 years old

In the third grade at Morrison School, Yung Wing studied Kate Lee's *A History of England*, *Colburn's Arithmetic Knowledge*, and English writing and handwriting. He completed the intellectual arithmetic manual and steadily improved his English language skills.

○ 图1-38 签署《香港宪章》的英国维多利亚女王，时年24岁

○ 图1-39 首任香港总督璞鼎查爵士，马礼逊学校赞助人之一

○ 图1-40 唐廷桂，今珠海唐家湾人。容闳马礼逊学校同学，15岁成为英国首任驻上海领事巴富尔翻译，后来成为怡和洋行总办，洋务运动的重要参与者

（16）1844年/容闳16岁

就读马礼逊学校四年级。完成英国历史课程；地理知识让容闳已经能勾勒西方主要国家的地理特征；开始学习力学，对牛顿的三大运动定律和万有引力定律等知识尤感兴趣。

马礼逊学校建在山顶，容闳常常从山顶眺望美丽的维多利亚港，倍感割地之伤。"登山眺望，自东至西，港口全境毕现。即此一处，已足见香港为中国南部形胜，无怪外人垂涎。且港口深阔，足为英国海军根据地。有此特点，故此岛终不我属，卒为英国有也。"（摘自《西学东渐记》）

1844/ at the age of 16

In the fourth grade at Morrison School, Yung Wing completed a course on British history and gained enough knowledge of geography that he was able to identify the geographical features of the major Western countries. He began to study mechanics and was very interested in learning about Newton's three laws of motion and the law of universal gravitation.

○ 图1-41　1844年的香港维多利亚港。容闳常常从学校所在山顶眺望美丽的港口

○ 图1-42　容闳就读的马礼逊学校部分老师。从左至右依次为：北美传教士哈巴安得、北美传教士麦嘉缔、美国传教士塞缪尔、伦敦会来华传教士美魏茶、北美传教士文惠廉

（17）1845年/容闳17岁

　　就读马礼逊学校五年级。9月，马礼逊学校举行公开考试，容闳现场英语作文《奇幻之旅》刊载于1845年11月1日《中国丛报》，他用娴熟的英语和丰富的想象，描绘了纽约的繁华和自己对西方文明的向往，没有想到一年之后，他的梦想成真。另一篇文章《改革》，刊登在《青年传教士资料库和主日学校传教杂志》上，重点论述了亨利八世的婚姻与当时宗教改革的关系。

　　是年，学习声乐课，每天唱歌半小时。

1845 / at the age of 17

　　Yung Wing was in his fifth year at Morrison. In September, Morrison School held a public exam, and his English essay "An Imaginary Voyage to New York and Up the Hudson," was published in *The Chinese Repository*. With his fluent English and creative mind, he described the prosperity of New York and his yearning for Western civilization. Little did he know that his dream would come true one year later.

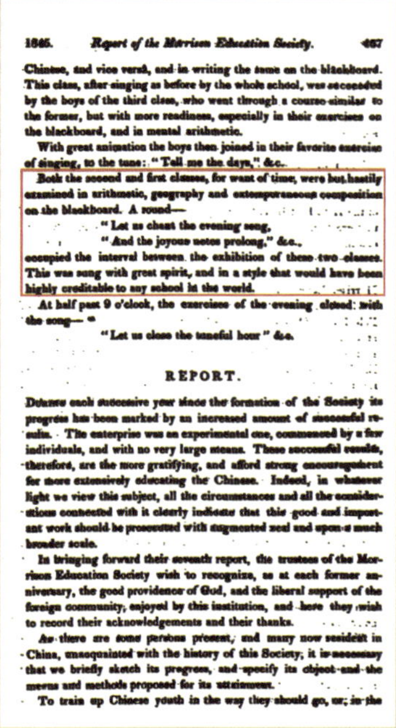
1845. Report of the Morrison Education Society. 467

Chinese, and vice versâ, and in writing the same on the blackboard. This class, after singing as before by the whole school, was seconded by the boys of the third class, who went through a course similar to the former, but with more readiness, especially in their exercises on the blackboard, and in mental arithmetic.

With great animation the boys then joined in their favorite exercise of singing, to the tune: "Tell me the days," &c.

Both the second and first classes, for want of time, were but hastily examined in arithmetic, geography and extemporaneous composition on the blackboard. A round—

"Let us chant the evening song,
"And the joyous notes prolong," &c.,

occupied the interval between the exhibition of these two classes. This was sung with great spirit, and in a style that would have been highly creditable to any school in the world.

At half past 9 o'clock, the exercises of the evening closed with the song—

"Let us close the tuneful hour" &c.

REPORT.

During each successive year since the formation of the Society its progress has been marked by an increased amount of successful results. The enterprise was an experimental one, commenced by a few individuals, and with no very large means. These successful results, therefore, are the more gratifying, and afford strong encouragement for more extensively educating the Chinese. Indeed, in whatever light we view this subject, all the circumstances and all the considerations connected with it clearly indicate that this good and important work should be prosecuted with augmented zeal and upon a much broader scale.

In bringing forward their seventh report, the trustees of the Morrison Education Society wish to recognize, as at each former anniversary, the good providence of God, and the liberal support of the foreign community, enjoyed by this institution, and here they wish to record their acknowledgements and their thanks.

As there are some persons present, and many now resident in China, unacquainted with the history of this Society, it is necessary that we briefly sketch its progress, and specify its object and the means and methods proposed for its attainment.

To train up Chinese youth in the way they should go, or, in the

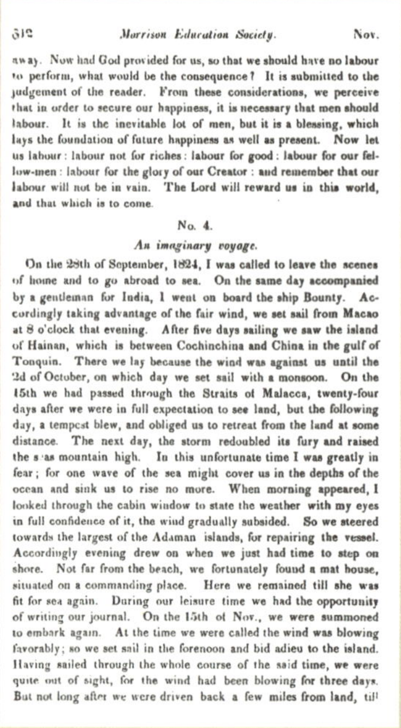
512 Morrison Education Society. Nov.

away. Now had God provided for us, so that we should have no labour to perform, what would be the consequence? It is submitted to the judgement of the reader. From these considerations, we perceive that in order to secure our happiness, it is necessary that men should labour. It is the inevitable lot of men, but it is a blessing, which lays the foundation of future happiness as well as present. Now let us labour: labour not for riches: labour for good: labour for our fellow-men: labour for the glory of our Creator: and remember that our labour will not be in vain. The Lord will reward us in this world, and that which is to come.

No. 4.

An imaginary voyage.

On the 28th of September, 1824, I was called to leave the scenes of home and to go abroad to sea. On the same day accompanied by a gentleman for India, I went on board the ship Bounty. Accordingly taking advantage of the fair wind, we set sail from Macao at 8 o'clock that evening. After five days sailing we saw the island of Hainan, which is between Cochinchina and China in the gulf of Tonquin. There we lay because the wind was against us until the 2d of October, on which day we set sail with a monsoon. On the 15th we had passed through the Straits of Malacca, twenty-four days after we were in full expectation to see land, but the following day, a tempest blew, and obliged us to retreat from the land at some distance. The next day, the storm redoubled its fury and raised the seas mountain high. In this unfortunate time I was greatly in fear; for one wave of the sea might cover us in the depths of the ocean and sink us to rise no more. When morning appeared, I looked through the cabin window to state the weather with my eyes in full confidence of it, the wind gradually subsided. So we steered towards the largest of the Adaman islands, for repairing the vessel. Accordingly evening drew on when we just had time to step on shore. Not far from the beach, we fortunately found a mat house, situated on a commanding place. Here we remained till she was fit for sea again. During our leisure time we had the opportunity of writing our journal. On the 15th of Nov., we were summoned to embark again. At the time we were called the wind was blowing favorably; so we set sail in the forenoon and bid adieu to the island. Having sailed through the whole course of the said time, we were quite out of sight, for the wind had been blowing for three days. But not long after we were driven back a few miles from land, till

○图1-43　9月24日，马礼逊教育会第七次年会期间，对容闳所在的第一期和第二期学员进行了即兴作文检测，左图为《马礼逊教育会第七次年度报告》对检测的记载（第三段），右图为刊载于1845年11月1日《中国丛报》容闳英语作文“An imaginary voyage”

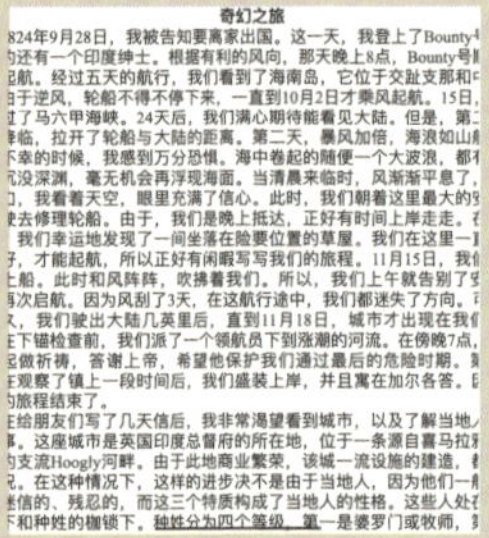
奇幻之旅

824年9月28日，我被告知要离家出国。这一天，我登上了Bounty
的还有一个印度绅士。根据有利的风向，那天晚上8点，Bounty号
起航。经过五天的航行，我们看到了海南岛，它位于交趾支那和
由于逆风，轮船不得不停下来，一直到10月2日才乘风起航。15日，
过了马六甲海峡。24天后，我们满心期待能看见大陆。但是，第
降临，拉开了轮船与大陆的距离。第二天，暴风加倍，海浪如山
不幸的时候，我感到万分恐惧。海中卷起的随便一个大波浪，都
沉没深渊，毫无机会再浮现海面。当清晨来临时，风渐渐平息了，
口，我看着天空，眼里充满了信心。此时，我们朝着这里最大的
驶去修理轮船。由于，我们是晚上抵达，正好有时间上岸走走。
我们幸运地发现了一间坐落在险要位置的草屋。我们在这里一
子，才能起航，所以正好有闲暇写写我们的旅程。11月15日，我
上船。此时和风阵阵，吹拂着我们。所以，我们上午就告别了
再次启航。因为风刮了3天，在这航行途中，我们都迷失了方向。
久，我们驶出大陆几英里后，直到11月18日，城市才出现在我
在下锚检查前，我们派了一个领航员下到涨潮的河流。在傍晚7点，
起做祈祷，答谢上帝，希望他保护我们通过最后的危险时期。
在观察了镇上一段时间后，我们盛装上岸，并且寓在加尔各答。
的旅程结束了。
在给朋友们写了几天信后，我非常渴望看到城市，以及了解当地
事。这座城市是英国印度总督府的所在地，位于一条源自喜马拉
的支流Hoogly河畔。由于此地商业繁荣，该城一流设施的建造，
况。在这种情况下，这样的进步决不是由于当地人，因为他们一
迷信的、残忍的，而这三个特质构成了当地人的性格。这些人处
下和种姓的枷锁下。种姓分为四个等级，第一是婆罗门或牧师，

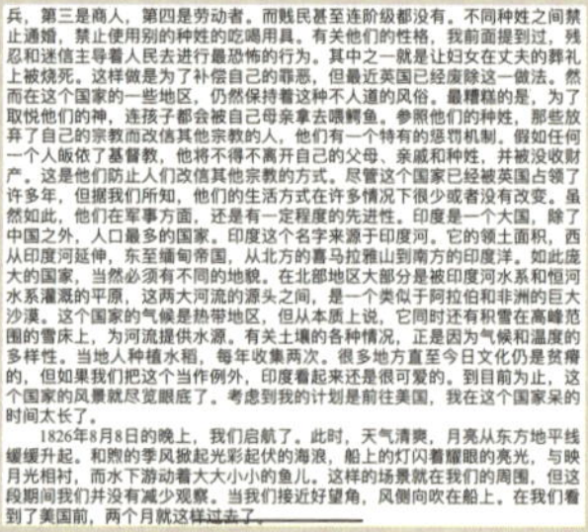
兵，第三是商人，第四是劳动者。而贱民甚至连阶级都没有。不同种姓之间禁止通婚，禁止使用别的种姓的吃喝用具。有关他们的性格，我前面提到过，残忍和迷信主导着人民去进行最恐怖的行为。其中之一就是让妇女在丈夫的葬礼上被烧死。这样做是为了补偿自己的罪恶，但最近英国已经废除这一做法。然而在这个国家的一些地区，仍然保持着这种不人道的风俗。最糟糕的是，为了取悦他们的神，连孩子都会被自己母亲拿去喂鳄鱼。参照他们的种姓，那些放弃了自己的宗教而改信其他宗教的人，他们有一个特有的惩罚机制。假如任何一个人皈依了基督教，他将不得不离开自己的父母、亲戚和种姓，并被没收财产。这是他们防止人们改信其他宗教的方式。尽管这个国家已经被英国占领了许多年，但据我们所知，他们的生活方式在许多情况下很少或者没有改变。虽然如此，他们在军事方面，还是有一定程度的先进性。印度是一个大国，除了中国之外，人口最多的国家。印度这个名字来源于印度河。它的领土面积，西从印度河延伸，东至缅甸帝国，从北方的喜马拉雅山到南方的印度洋。如此庞大的国家，当然必须有不同的地貌。在北部地区大部分是被印度河水系和恒河水系灌溉的平原，这两大河流的源头之间，是一个类似于阿拉伯和非洲的巨大沙漠。这个国家的气候是热带地区，但从本质上说，它同时还有积雪在高峰范围的雪床上，为河流提供水源。有关土壤的各种情况，正是因为气候和温度的多样性。当地人种植水稻，每年收集两次。很多地方直至今日文化仍是贫瘠的，但如果我们把这个当作例外，印度看起来还是很可爱的。到目前为止，这个国家的风景就尽览眼底了。考虑到我的计划是前往美国，我在这个国家呆的时间太长了。

1826年8月8日的晚上，我们启航了。此时，天气清爽，月亮从东方地平线缓缓升起。和煦的季风掀起光彩起伏的海浪，船上的灯闪着耀眼的亮光，与映月光相衬，而水下游动着大大小小的鱼儿。这样的场景就在我们的周围，但这段期间我们并没有减少观察。当我们接近好望角，风侧向吹在船上。在我们看到了美国前，两个月就这样过去了。

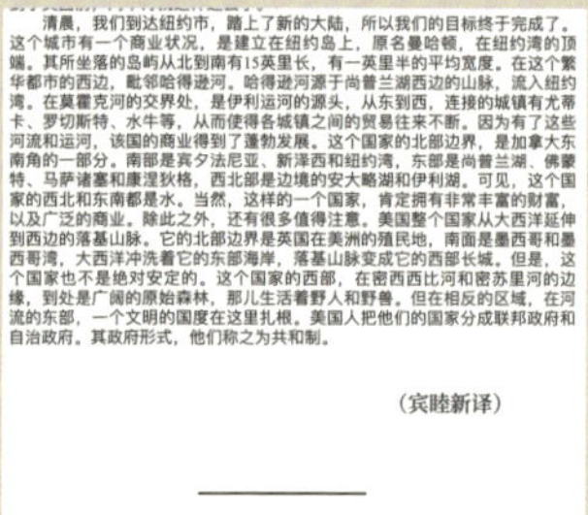
清晨，我们到达纽约市，踏上了新的大陆，所以我们的目标终于完成了。这个城市有一个商业状况，是建立在纽约岛上，原名曼哈顿，在纽约湾的顶端。其所坐落的岛屿从北到南有15英里长，有一英里半的平均宽度。在这个繁华都市的西边，毗邻哈得逊河。哈得逊河源于尚普兰湖西边的山脉，流入纽约湾。在莫霍克河的交界处，是伊利运河的源头，从东到西，连接的城镇有尤蒂卡、罗切斯特、水牛等，从而使得各城镇之间的贸易往来不断。因为有了这些河流和运河，该国的商业得到了蓬勃发展。这个国家的北部边界，是加拿大东南角的一部分。南部是宾夕法尼亚、新泽西和纽约湾，东部是尚普兰湖、佛蒙特、马萨诸塞和康涅狄格，西北部是边境的安大略湖和伊利湖。可见，这个国家的西北和东南都是水。当然，这样的一个国家，肯定拥有非常丰富的财富，以及广泛的商业。除此之外，还有很多值得注意。美国整个国家从大西洋延伸到西边的落基山脉。它的北部边界是英国在美洲的殖民地，南面是墨西哥和墨西哥湾，大西洋冲洗着它的东部海岸，落基山脉变成它的西部长城。但是，这个国家也不是绝对安定的。这个国家的西部，在密西西比河和密苏里河的边缘，到处是广阔的原始森林，那儿生活着野人和野兽。但在相反的区域，在河流的东部，一个文明的国度在这里扎根。美国人把他们的国家分成联邦政府和自治政府。其政府形式，他们称之为共和制。

（宾睦新译）

○图1-44　图为容闳英语作文“An imaginary voyage”，中文翻译“奇幻之旅”（宾睦新译）

（18）1846年/容闳18岁

就读马礼逊学校六年级。开始学习代数，初步掌握了一次和二次方程、根、乘方以及二项式定理，增加了翻译课程。9月，布朗校长因妻子病重需回美国治疗，希望带几名学生随行留学二年，留学费用由在香港的苏格兰商人康白尔，香港《德臣西报》主笔、苏格兰人萧德锐和美国商人里奇等人资助。"当布朗先生布告游美方针时，予首先起立，次黄胜，次黄宽"（摘自《西学东渐记》）。容闳、黄胜（今珠海东岸村人）、黄宽（今珠海东岸村人）的这一决定，不仅改变了自己的一生，也改变了许多中国人的一生。

1846//at the age of 18

Yung Wing was in the sixth grade at Morrison School. In September of that year, due to the serious illness of Brown's wife, Mr. Brown decided to return to the U.S. Yung Wing writes that "When he [Mr. Brown] requested those who wished to accompany him to the States to signify it by rising, I was the first one on my feet. Huang Kuan was the second, followed by Huang Sheng" (from *My Life in China and America*).

o 图1-45 1846年的香港铜锣湾

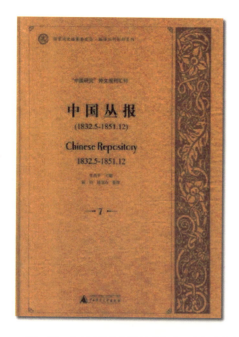

o 图1-46 《中国丛报》第16卷报道了布朗夫妇携带黄胜、容闳、黄宽赴美留学的消息

第二章　负笈重洋

(1847-1854)

Journeying across the seas to learn

（19）1847年/容闳19岁

1月4日，与黄胜、黄宽一起随布朗夫妇，从广州黄埔港乘"亨特利思号"帆船赴美留学。三位敢为人先的珠海少年勇敢迈出的步伐开启了中国百年留学大潮的序幕，成为中国人接受完整西式教育、系统学习西方科学的发端。他们的壮举为"日之将夕，悲风骤至"的晚清社会增添一抹亮色。《友谊报》《密西西比州浸会教》等美国报纸报道了布朗携容闳等人赴美留学及抵达纽约的相关消息，报道称容闳等三人为马礼逊学校最优秀的学生。

历经98天惊涛骇浪中的颠簸穿行，4月12日抵达纽约港。途经大西洋圣赫勒拿岛时，容闳特意上岛拜谒拿破仑墓，抚今吊古，折墓边柳枝带至美国，1854年容闳在纽约阿朋学校再见当年柳枝已成大树，郁郁葱葱，万千垂柳。

4月，偶遇耶鲁大学校长。"自纽约乘舟赴纽黑文，以机会之佳，得晤耶鲁大学校长谭君，数年之后，竟得毕业此校，当时固非敢有此奢望也。"（摘自《西学东渐记》）

入读马萨诸塞州孟松学校，与黄宽、黄胜成为这个学校最早的中国学生。

1847/at the age of 19

On January 4th, Yung Wing, Huang Sheng and Huang Kuan boarded the sailing ship *Huntress* from Huangpu Port in Guangzhou, accompanying Brown and his wife to study in America. In doing so, the three teenagers from Zhuhai were the first Chinese students to study abroad, and the first to accept Western education and Western science.

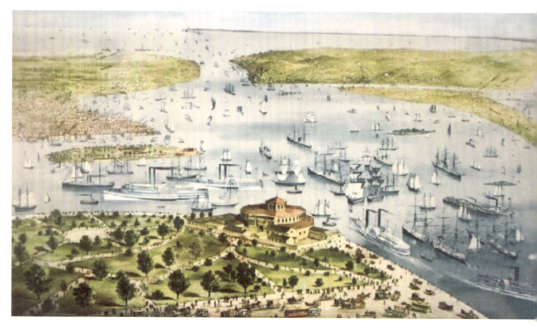

o 图2-1　1847年的纽约港，容闳在此踏上美国

o 图2-2　左图为容闳嫡孙容永成手抚"亨特利思号"帆船模型，在新加坡家中向笔者讲述祖父
的故事。右图为布朗岳父巴脱拉脱牧师日记中关于容闳一行初到美国的记载

（20）1848年/容闳20岁

　　孟松学校学习。"彼时美国尚无高等中学，仅有预备学校，孟松即预备学校中之最著名者。全国好学之士，莫不负笈远来，肄业此校，为入大学之预备。"（摘自《西学东渐记》）

　　居住在布朗家中，得到布朗母亲细心的生活照料。学校一年级设置数学、文法、生理学、心理学、拉丁文，希腊文和哲学等课程。与心理学课老师勃朗和夫君麦克林博士成为一生挚友。"夫妇二人，待予咸极诚挚，每值放假，必邀予过其家。及予入耶路大学肄业，处境甚窘，赖渠夫妇资助之力尤多，归国后，彼此犹音问不绝。及再至美国，复下榻其家。马萨诸塞州有此良友，令人每念不忘。一八七二年，予携第一批留学生游美时，即赁屋邻麦博士，公假期常得与吾友把晤也。"（摘自《西学东渐记》）

　　是年秋，黄胜因病回国。

1848/at the age of 20

　　Yung Wing enrolled in the Monson Academy in Massachusetts, along with Huang Kuan and Huang Sheng, becoming the first Chinese students to attend the school. He writes that "At that time, there were no higher secondary schools in the United States, only preparatory schools, and Monson was the most famous of them. Students from all over the country came here to study in preparation for entering university." (from *My Life in China and America*)

o 图2-3　19世纪的孟松小镇及孟松学校

MERRICK, FAY & CO'S STRAW WORKS.

GREEN'S HOTEL.

A.N.L.N.P.R. Station
1. Central Block.
2. Towne's Block.
3. Barton's Block.
4. Green's Block.
5. Green's Hotel, D. G. Green Owner & Proprietor.
6. Cushman's Hotel, L. G. Cushman, Owner & Proprietor.
7. Congregational Church
8. Methodist　"
9. St. Patricks R. C. "
10. Monson Academy
11. School Buildings.
12. Monson National Bank, C. W. Holmes, President.
　　K. F. Morris, Cashier
13. Merrick, Fay & Co., Manufacturers of Straw Goods
14. Reynolds' Mills, (Fancy Casimeres).
　　J. L. Reynolds,　R. M. & T. Reynolds.

15. S.F.Cushman, Ma
16. D.W.Ellis & Son,
17. C. W. Holmes, Jr.,
18. W. N. Flynt & Co
19. G.W.Burdick, Bla
　　Retail Ice Dealer
20. H.R.Glynn, Ca
21. Chas E Smith, Ha
22. A Squier, Lumbe
　　Post Office, Town
　　Chas Fowler, Tow
　　Geo R Grout, Towne
　　G W Andrews, D
　　Duchette & Beox,
　　ing Goods, Barton
　　Eugene F Willis,
　　Furnishing Goods,
　　Chas R Dudley,
　　Block

MONSO

O.H. BAILEY & CO.

Casimeres.
-Casimeres.

Wholesale &

M.
Merchandise
y, Notions &c

nts' Furnish

Gents

gent, Green's

MASS.

SHER & BOSTON

REYNOLDS WOOLEN MILLS.

Phoebe Hinsdale Brown and her husband, Timothy, who was a painter and carpenter, lived in this house at 103 Main Street. In 1818, she wrote a poem which became the well-known hymn, "I Love to Steal Awhile Away." She had four little children and a sick sister living in the only finished room. The Thomas J. Whiting family is pictured in front of the house around 1855.

Phoebe Brown used to walk at dusk to escape the cares of the day and to admire the fragrant fruits and flowers in a neighbor's lovely garden. Rebuked for intruding, Phoebe wrote a poem as an apology. The American Tract Society publication *The History of an Indian Woman,* or *Religion Exemplified in the Life of Poor Sarah,* about a Native American who lived at Shenipsit Lake, is attributed to her. (Courtesy of Watkinson Library, Trinity College, Hartford, Connecticut.)

○ 图2-4　上图为布朗在孟松的家。下图为他的母亲。容闳初到美国居住于此，与老人感情深厚

（21）1849年/容闳21岁

就读孟松学校二年级。校长海门毕业于耶鲁大学，对三个中国学生特别厚爱，期望他们能够学成归国，有所建树。受其影响，容闳酷爱英国文学。

面临美国学习生涯的第一次艰难选择。

随着两年资助期限临近，容闳耶鲁之梦越发强烈，虽然学费问题悬而未决，九月之后，毅然开始大学备考科目学习。苏格兰商人康白尔提出如转往其母校爱丁堡大学学医，可以继续资助。容闳婉拒，随后又婉拒毕业成为传教士等有条件资助。此时其内心已经以身许国，知道一旦签约，必受束缚，将来即使有报效祖国的更好机会，也只能坐失机遇。"予之对于此等条件，则不轻诺。予虽贫，自由所固有。他日竟学，无论何业，将择其最有益于中国者为之……若陷于一业，则范围甚狭，有用之身，必致无用，且传道固佳，未必即为造福中国独一无二之事业。"（摘自《西学东渐记》）

1849/ at the age of 21

In his second year at Monson Academy, Yung Wing faced his first difficult decision in his American academic career. Originally, his funding for studying abroad was only for two years. There was no funding for him to go to college. As his return date approached, Yung Wing's dream of attending Yale grew stronger.

o 图2-5 4月15日，容闳致函好
友、当时在中国的美国人卫三畏，
请卫三畏代他和叔叔容名彰商议他
继续留在美国的事，转请叔叔向母
亲解释。同时请卫三畏雇用他的哥
哥容阿林

Rev. Charles Hammond

查尔斯·海门先生

o 图2-6 孟松所属的新英格兰地区是美国殖民地时期最早开发和定居的地区之一，其独特的精
神文化深刻影响了容闳的思想，后来这个地区也成为中国留学生的主要区域。左图为新英格兰地
区地图。右图为容闳在孟松学校读书期间的校长海门

Dr. Arnold of Rugby, he aimed to build character in his pupils and not to convert them into walking encyclopedias, or intelligent parrots. It was through him that I was introduced to Addison, Goldsmith, Dickens, Sir Walter Scott, the Edinburgh Reviews, Macaulay and Shakespeare, which formed the bulk of my reading while in Monson.

During my first year in the Monson Academy, I had no idea of taking a collegiate course. It was well understood that I was to return to China at the end of 1849, and the appropriation was made to suit such a plan. In the fall of 1848, after Wong Shing—the eldest of the three of us—had returned to China on account of his poor health, Wong Foon and myself, who were left behind to continue our studies for another year, frequently met to talk over future plans for the end of the prescribed time. We both decided finally to stay in this country to continue our studies, but the question arose, who was going to back us financially after 1849? This was the Gordian Knot. We concluded to consult Mr. Hammond and Mr. Brown on the subject. They both decided to have the matter referred to

曷足贵哉！海君之为教授，盖能深合阿那博士所云教育之本旨者也。予在孟松学校时，曾诵习多数英国之文集，皆海君所亲授者。

在孟松之第一年，予未敢冀入大学。盖予等出发时，仅以二年为限，一八四九年即须回国也。三人中，以黄胜齿为最长。一八四八年秋，黄胜以病归国，仅予与黄宽二人。居恒晤谈，辄讨及二年后之方针。予本志，固深愿继续求学。惟一八四九年后，将恃何人资助予等学费，此问题之困难，殆不啻古所谓"戈登结"，几乎无人能解者，则亦惟有商之于海门校长及勃朗君耳。幸得二君厚意，允为函询香港资助予等之人。追得覆书，则谓二年后如予二人愿至英国之苏格兰省之爱丁堡大学习专门科者，则彼等仍可继续资助云云。予等蒙其慷慨解囊，历久不倦，诚为可感。嗣予等互竞相进止，黄宽决计二年后至苏格兰补此学额。予则誓欲入耶鲁大学，故愿仍留美。议既定，于是黄宽学费，已可无恐。予于一八四九年后，借何资以求学，此问题固仍悬而未决也。亦惟有泰然处之，任予运命之自然，不复为无益之虑。

学费问题

o 图2-7 容闳回忆录中关于
萌生报考大学想法的记载

（22）1850年/容闳22岁

朝夕相处10年的同窗好友黄宽（今珠海东岸村人）接受康白尔资助，转赴英国爱丁堡大学学医，成为近代中国留欧获得博士学位第一人和中国西医的开山鼻祖。

得益于布朗牧师的帮助，萨伐那妇女协会同意资助学费。容闳立刻赴考，终于成为耶鲁大学首位中国学生。后来，他的两个儿子也从这所大学毕业，他带领的首批中国官派留美幼童，近1/4就读这所学校。

是年，在耶鲁大学例行举办的新老学生橄榄球比赛中，容闳关键时刻触地得分，取得建校以来新生队首次胜利。

1850/ at the age of 22

Yung Wing graduated from Monson Academy. His close friend Huang Kuan received financial support and transferred to the University of Edinburgh to study medicine. Huang became a Chinese pioneer in Western medicine. Fortunately, just before his exams, Yung Wing was able to obtain funding, and was successfully admitted to Yale College, becoming its first Chinese student.

○ 图2-8 19世纪的耶鲁大学

○图2-9　左图为1850年美国人口普查中含有容闳信息的档案。右图为资助容闳读大学的萨伐那妇女协会旧址

○图2-10　转赴英国留学的黄宽和19世纪的爱丁堡大学

○图2-11　左图为黄宽于爱丁堡大学的个人记录（1850）。右图为位于今珠海东岸村的黄宽故居

（23）1851年/容闳23岁

就读耶鲁大学一年级。初入校门，拖着长辫、穿着长袍马褂，形象怪异。很快剪掉辫子，换上西装马甲。容闳非常喜欢耶鲁，在给朋友卫三畏的信中写道："耶鲁正沉浸在雄心勃发的氛围当中，我认为雄心壮志可成就大业，我更多的是被这种氛围感染，我非常喜欢他对我的影响。"

由于基础薄弱，大一异常辛苦，通宵达旦学习，尤其为数学所困，特别畏惧微积分，常常考试不及格，总担心着被斥退或留级。第一学期平均分仅达到合格。"在第一年级时，读书恒至夜半，日间亦无闲暇游戏运动，体魄日就羸弱，曾因精力不支，请假赴东温若休息一星期，乃能继续求学。"（摘自《西学东渐记》）。

1851/ at the age of 23

As a freshman at Yale College, Yung Wing stood out with his peculiar appearance, wearing a long robe with his long braid dragging behind his head. However, he quickly cut off his braid and donned a Western suit. Due to his weak academic foundation, Yung Wing struggled with mathematics and frequently failed exams. He worried about being dismissed or held back.

○ 图2-12 12月25日，容闳致卫三畏信件，叙述他的学习生活以及他对家乡亲人的牵挂和思念

○ 图2-13 19世纪中叶的耶鲁大学图书馆，容闳常常在这里通宵达旦学习

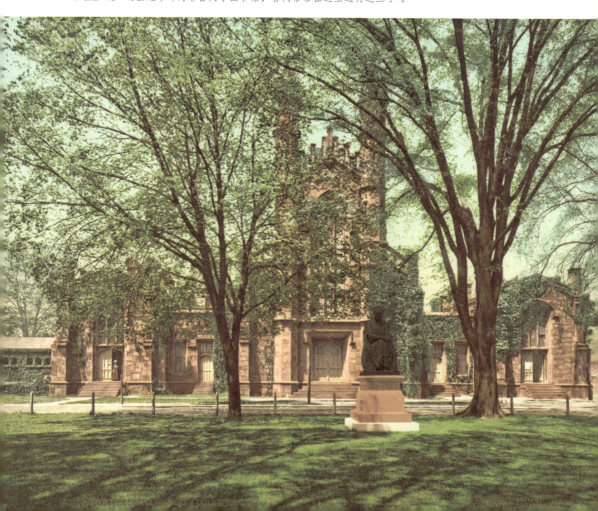

（24）1852年/容闳24岁

就读耶鲁大学二年级，英文论文写作竞赛连获两次一等奖，数学分数落差终于被英文作文高分拉平。当地《里士满日报》报道了这个中国学生获得英语竞赛作文最高奖项的消息。香港报纸也进行转载。"容（闳）异服异俗，颇受人笑。其年，容两得班中英文第一奖，其后无敢揶揄之者矣。"（摘自《胡适留学日记》）

是年，耶鲁大学与哈佛大学首场赛艇对抗赛拉开帷幕。容闳特别喜欢这项活动，成为耶鲁大学辛利亚赛艇队19名队员之一，队员称其名"威风"。棒球、合唱，也是他当时喜欢的文体项目。

年底开始直到毕业，为同寝室同学经营伙食，勤工俭学，基本解决生活费用。

1852/ at the age of 24

As a sophomore at Yale College, Yung Wing won two first prizes in English composition, which finally balanced out his poor math scores. The local *Richmond Daily News* reported on the news of this Chinese student receiving the highest award in English.

Falling of a Wall—Probable Loss of Life.

CHICAGO, May 12.—The entire front of a large brick warehouse on Market street, filled with corn, belonging to C. M. Read, of Erie, fell into the street to-day, crushing it to the depth of 20 feet. It is feared several persons are buried under the ruins.

Selden, Withers & Co., Bankers, of Washington city, have taken $500,000 six per cent. bonds of the city of Wheeling.

At the Annual Exhibition of the Junior Class at Yale College last month, the highest prize for *English* composition, was awarded to Yung Wing, a native Chinese.

A boy died in New York, on Sunday, from eating ice cream and smoking a cigar immediately afterwards.

A clerk of one of the Boston markets recently seized thirty-six carcasses of veal, totally unfit for any person to eat, and which had been sold to a sausage-maker for thirty cents a carcass.

○ 图2-14　5月15日，《里士满日报》关于容闳获奖的报道，报道称：上个月在耶鲁大学第3年级年度展览会上，英语作文最高奖项授予了中国人容闳

○ 图2-15　赛艇和棒球是容闳在大学期间最喜欢的两项运动。图为当时的耶鲁大学棒球队

（25）1853年/ 容闳25岁

就读耶鲁大学三年级，成为"兄弟会"藏书楼管理员，结交了很多朋友，经济问题也彻底解决，不再举债，并托人给母亲带去25元钱。同时，各科成绩大为提高，新大陆自由之精神、活泼之思想也渐渐地融入了他的血液。

在美国的大学生活虽然如鱼得水，但中西文明的巨大差距时时令他耿耿于怀，国家孱弱、百姓愚昧更令他倍感此生负荷极重，使命感油然而生。"予当修业期内，中国之腐败情形，时触予怀，迨末年而尤甚。每一念及，辄为之怏怏不乐……更念中国国民，身受无限痛苦，无限压制。此痛苦与压制，在彼未受教育之人，竟浑然不知，毫无感觉。"（摘自《西学东渐记》）

1853/ at the age of 25

In his junior year at Yale, he earned money as the fraternity's librarian. His financial pressures were solved. Although he was like a fish in water in American university life, the huge gap between China and Western civilizations always lingered in his mind, making him feel an immense burden due to the weakness of his country and the ignorance of the people.

○ 图2-16 美国19世纪欣欣向荣的工业小镇

○ 图2-17 6月26日，容闳手写的中英文偈语"善似青松恶似花，如今眼前不及他，有朝一日霜雪下，只见青松不见花"

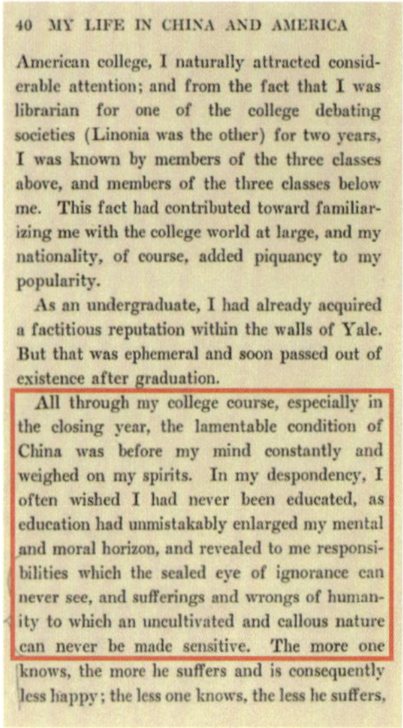

40 MY LIFE IN CHINA AND AMERICA

American college, I naturally attracted considerable attention; and from the fact that I was librarian for one of the college debating societies (Linonia was the other) for two years, I was known by members of the three classes above, and members of the three classes below me. This fact had contributed toward familiarizing me with the college world at large, and my nationality, of course, added piquancy to my popularity.

As an undergraduate, I had already acquired a factitious reputation within the walls of Yale. But that was ephemeral and soon passed out of existence after graduation.

All through my college course, especially in the closing year, the lamentable condition of China was before my mind constantly and weighed on my spirits. In my despondency, I often wished I had never been educated, as education had unmistakably enlarged my mental and moral horizon, and revealed to me responsibilities which the sealed eye of ignorance can never see, and sufferings and wrongs of humanity to which an uncultivated and callous nature can never be made sensitive. The more one knows, the more he suffers and is consequently less happy; the less one knows, the less he suffers.

予于一八五四年毕业。同班中毕业者，共九十八人。以中国人而毕业于美国第一等之大学校，实自予始。以故美国人对予感情至佳。时校中中国学生，绝无仅有，易于令人注目。又因予尝任兄弟会藏书楼中司书之职二年，故相识之人尤多。同校前后三级中之学生，稔予者几过半。故余熟悉美国情形，而于学界中交游尤广。予在校时，名誉颇佳。于今思之，亦无甚关系。浮云过眼，不过博得一时虚荣耳。

第一个中国毕业生

予当修业期内，中国之腐败情形，时触予怀，迨末年而尤甚。每一念及，辄为之怏怏不乐，转愿不受此良教育之为愈。盖既受教育，则予心中之理想既高，而道德之范围亦广，遂觉此身负荷极重，若在毫无知识时代，转不之觉也。更念中国国民，身受无限痛苦，无限压制。此痛苦与压制，在彼未受教育之人，亦转毫无感觉，初不知其为痛苦与压制也。故予尝谓知识益高者，痛苦亦多，而快乐益少。反之，

○ 图2-18 容闳回忆录中关于当时忧国忧民情怀的记载

（26）1854年/容闳26岁

以优异成绩从耶鲁大学荣誉毕业，获文学学士学位，成为第一个毕业于美国大学的中国人。毕业前夕，未来人生规划已成熟于胸，确定返回中国，推动留学教育计划。同班同学卡廷在毕业赠言中祝福容闳："我真的希望您为她所立的大计划终会实现，而您将在您的同胞的生活中成为一位伟大、优良和有用之人。"

"予意以为予之一身，既受此文明之教育，则当使后予之人，亦享此同等之利益。以西方之学术，灌输于中国，使中国日趋于文明富强之境。予后来之事业，盖皆以此为标强，专心致志以为之。"（摘自《西学东渐记》）

写下中英文毕业赠言："大人者不失其赤子之心。"这最终成为他一生心路历程的真实写照。1854年10月3日，《新奥尔良日报》报道了容闳荣誉毕业于耶鲁大学和获得美国护照的消息。报道称容闳是一个极有学习天赋的年轻人，已经在美国和我们朝夕相处了八年，他将要回到中国。

是年，11月13日，从纽约港启程回国。

1854/ at the age of 26

Yung Wing graduated with honors from Yale University, becoming the first Chinese person to graduate from an American university. On November 13th, Yung Wing departed for China. "Before the close of my last year in college, I had already sketched out what I should do. I was determined that the rising generation of China should enjoy the same educational advantages that I had enjoyed-that through western education, China might be regenerated, become enlightened and powerful. (from *My Life in China and America*)

o 图2-19　耶鲁大学毕业纪念册中的容闳毕业照和他手写的"尽人事而听天命"的中英文手迹

o 图2-20　耶鲁大学1854年毕业生留言簿和容闳毕业册中为同学中英文留言4张

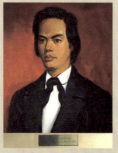

o 图2-21　左图为耶鲁大学保存的容闳毕业照。右图为美国女画家朱迪丝·里夫根据照片所作的油画，至今仍然陈列在耶鲁大学访问中心

o 图2-22　10月3日《新奥尔良时报》关于容闳耶鲁大学荣誉毕业和即将返回中国的报道

第三章　学成报国

Serving the Country

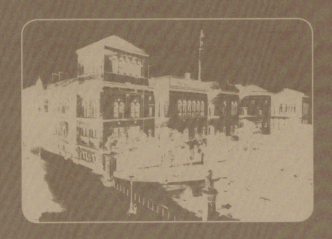

（27）1855年/容闳27岁

经过154天航行，回到阔别十年的祖国。在香港靠岸后，容闳首先拜访资助他学习的《德臣西报》总编萧德锐。

回到故乡南屏，探望年过半百的母亲。"予见母无恙，胸中感谢之心，达于极点，喜极欲涕，此种状记，实非语言笔墨所能形容。"（摘自《西学东渐记》）

短暂逗留后，便前往广州补习生疏多年的母语。其间，目睹两广总督叶名琛屠杀天地会起义会众的暴行，更坚定了他改造中国的决心。

1855/at the age of 27

After a 154-day voyage, he arrived in Hong Kong and paid a visit to Andrew Shortrede who had sponsored his studies and who was the editor-in-chief of *The China Mail.* Upon returning to his hometown of Nanping, he visited his mother who was already in her fifties. After a brief stay, he went to Guangzhou to brush up on his mother tongue, which he had not used in many years.

○ 图3-1　19世纪的广州城

十有四，计去予失怙时，凡二十四年。予母逝时，予适在
上海，未能见一面，实为终天遗憾。

一八五五年予居粤中，与美教士富文
(Vrooman)君同寓，地名"咸虾栏"，与行
刑场颇近。场在城外西南隅，邻珠江之滨。
予之寓此，除补习汉文而外，他无所事。以予久居美洲，
于本国语言，几尽忘之，至是乃渐复其旧。不及六月，竟
能重操粤语，惟唇舌间尚觉生硬耳。至予之汉文，乃于一
八四六年游美之前所习者，为时不过四年。以习汉文，学
期实为至短，根基之浅，自不待言。故今日之温习，颇极
困难，进步极缓。夫文字之与语言，在英文中虽间有不同
之点，究不若中国之悬殊特甚。以中国之文字而论，辉煌
华丽，变化万端，虽应用普及全国，而文字之发音，则南
北互异，东西悬殊。至于语言，则尤庞杂不可究诘。如福
建、江苏、安徽等省，即一省之中，亦有无数不同之方
言。每值甲乙两地人相遇，设各操其乡谈，则几如异国之
人，彼此不能通解。此乃中国语言文字上特别困难之处。

重新学习
中国语文

○ 图3-2　左图为容闳回忆录中关于回国初期到广州学习汉语的情况。右图中间的标红部分为广
州的咸虾栏，容闳曾在这里学习半年汉语

（28）1856年/容闳28岁

汉语能力恢复，着手寻找合适的职位。"此非仅为家人衣食，欲有所籍手，达于维新中国之目的，谋食亦谋道也。"（摘自《西学东渐记》）

第一份工作是在广州担任美国驻华公使伯驾私人秘书，希望借此结识清廷官员，获得实现留学教育计划的机会。因伯驾对其计划不理解，三个月后辞职。第二份工作是在香港最高法院任传译员，希望成为第一个在香港法庭执业的中国人，遭到被英国律师垄断的香港法律界抵制，8月，辞职离港。此间结识后来成为太平天国干王的洪仁玕。第三份工作是在上海江海关翻译处任头等通事，薪酬优厚，但是对留学教育计划毫无帮助，再次辞职。总税务司英国人李泰国亲自挽留，承诺将月俸从75两提高到200两白银，不为所动。

一年三易其职，难免被人认为好高骛远，不切实际。然而燕雀安知鸿鹄之志："予之生于斯世，既非为哺啜而来，予之受此教育，尤非易易；则含辛茹苦所得者，又安能不望其实行于中国耶，一旦遇有机会，能多用我一分学问，即多获一分效果，此岂为一人利益计，抑欲谋全中国之幸福也！"（摘自《西学东渐记》）

1856/at the age of 28

Yung Wing began to search for suitable employment. His first job was as a secretary to the American Envoy to China in Guangzhou. His second job was in Hong Kong's Supreme Court. His third job was as the head translator at the Customs Bureau in Shanghai. After changing jobs three times in one year, he was seen as unrealistic. He wrote, "We are not called into being simply to drudge for an animal existence. I had to work hard for my education, and I felt that I ought to make most of what little I had, not so much to benefit myself individually, as to make it a blessing common to my race." (from *My Life in China and America*)

o 图3-3　容闳工作过的广州美国领事馆

○ 图3-4 容闳工作过的香港高等法院（左）和上海江海关（右）

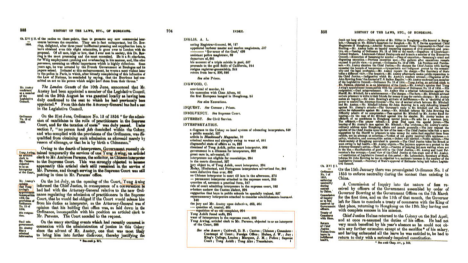

○ 图3-5 《德臣西报》关于容闳出任香港最高法院传译员的相关报道

（29）　1857年/容闳29岁

在上海以翻译为生，结识徐润、郑观应等香山买办和李善兰、华蘅芳、徐寿、张斯桂等当时饱读西洋书籍的西学人士，因翻译宝顺洋行"行主"的墓志铭名声大著，所译英文被镌刻在墓碑上。

年底，入职宝顺洋行，尝试积财以实现他的留学教育计划。

1857/at the age of 29

In Shanghai, he made a living as a translator and gained great fame for his skilled translation of a Chinese eulogy for the owner of Dent & Co., a foreign trading company. At the end of the year, seeking to raise enough money to finance his study abroad program, he joined Dent & Co.

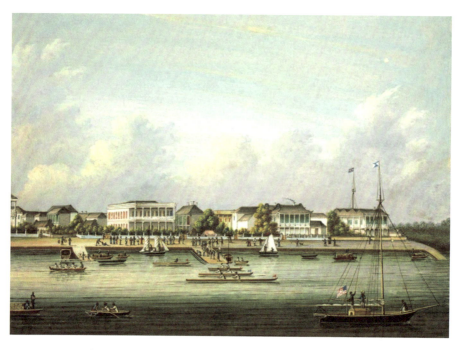

o 图3-6　19世纪中期的上海逐渐成为全国贸易中心

o 图3-7　容闳工作过的上海宝顺洋行

（30）1858年/容闳30岁

　　拒绝宝顺洋行总经理韦伯让其前往日本担任宝顺洋行驻长崎代理处买办职位，认为买办是"洋行中奴隶之首领"，辱没耶鲁大学声誉，韦伯赞叹容闳"容某虽贫，傲骨殊稜稜"。

　　是年，黄河泛滥，灾民涌至上海附近，撰写英文通告向旅居上海外国人募集两万银元，并以中国资金筹集委员会名义撰写英文致谢信刊登在上海英文报纸《上海邮报》和《中国之友》上。

　　是年，容闳同学黄胜（今珠海东岸村人）等人在香港创办了中国人自办的第一张近代报纸《香港中外新报》。

1858/at the age of 30

　　He refused an offer from Dent & Co.'s general manager Webb to go to Nagasaki, Japan as the company's comprador, believing that the position of comprador "is associated with all that is menial, and that as a graduate of Yale," he could not tarnish Yale University's reputation. Weber praised Yung Wing, stating that "Yung Wing is poor but proud. Poverty and pride usually go together, hand and hand."

o 图3-8 左图为黄胜，和容闳一道留学美国，后来成为香港首位华人太平绅士。右图为黄胜等创办的近代中国第一家中文日报《香港中外新报》

different races of the world into one brotherhood.

My friend Tsang Kee Foo afterwards introduced me to the head or manager of Messrs. Dent & Co., who kindly offered me a position in his firm as comprador in Nagasaki, Japan, soon after that country was opened to foreign trade. I declined the situation, frankly and plainly stating my reason, which was that the compradorship, though lucrative, is associated with all that is menial, and that as a graduate of Yale, one of the leading colleges in America, I could not think of bringing discredit to my Alma Mater, for which I entertained the most profound respect and reverence, and was jealous of her proud fame. What would the college and my class-mates think of me, if they should hear that I was a comprador—the head servant of servants in an English establishment? I said

Digitized by Google

78　MY LIFE IN CHINA AND AMERICA

there were cases when a man from stress of circumstances may be compelled to play the part of a menial for a shift, but I was not yet reduced to that strait, though I was poor financially. I told him I would prefer to travel for the firm as its agent in the interior and correspond directly

倡，乃得实行。予尝谓世上之事，殆如蛛网之牵丝，不能预定交友之中，究何人能解吾毕生之结。即如予之因曾（继甫）〔当为寄圃〕而识李，因李而识曾（文正），因曾而予之教育计划乃得告成，又因予之教育计画告成，而中西学术萃于一堂，充类至义之尽，将来世界成为一家，不可谓非由此滥觞。则又如蛛网之到处牵连，不知以何处为止境也。

予因曾继甫，旋识宝顺公司（Dent & Co.）之西经理。经理遇予颇厚，欲命予至日本长崎为其分公司之买办，时日本与各国通商尚未久也。予则婉辞不就其职，且实告以故，谓：

〔拒绝充当洋行买办〕

"买办之俸虽优，然操业近卑鄙。予固美国领袖学校之毕业生，故予极重视母校，尊之敬之，不敢使予之所予于母校之名誉少有辱没。以买办之身分，不过洋行中奴隶之首领耳。以予而为洋行中奴隶之首领，则使予之母校及诸同学闻之，对予将生如何之感情耶？人虽有时困于经济，不得不屈就贱役，为稻粱谋，第予之贫乏尚未至此。设君果任予以事者，则予甚愿为公司代表，至内地一行。如是则予不至以金钱之故而牺牲尊贵之身分。予苟得代表公司以收买丝茶，无论或给常薪，或给用费，似较任奴隶首领为佳也。"予言时，予友曾君亦在座。曾君粗解英语，于予言虽知之不详，固已得其概略。予语毕，乃先辞出，以待彼二人协商。曾君后出语予，谓绘白（Webb）〔通译作韦伯〕（即该公司之经理）评予曰："容某虽贫，傲骨殊稜稜。"天下贫者之与傲骨，乃往往长相伴而不相离也。谈判后数日，曾君告

o 图3-9 容闳回忆录中关于拒绝担任洋行买办的记载

（31）1859年/容闳31岁

3月，受宝顺洋行委派前往苏州、杭州、荆州、南昌、湘潭、长沙、汉口等地，调查长江沿岸丝茶生产销售出口等情况，此行横跨五省，历时七个月，沿途所见所闻，使其对中国国情民情有了深刻了解，对汉口印象深刻。虽然汉口在太平军占领之后已成一片焦土。"当予至时，商业已渐恢复，被焚之区，亦从新建筑……予知不久汉口之商业发达，居民繁盛，必将驾芝加哥、圣路易而上之。"（摘自《西学东渐记》）回上海后，撰写并向宝顺洋行提交《产茶区域之初次调查》。

1859/at the age of 31

In March, Yung Wing was dispatched to Suzhou, Hangzhou, Jingzhou, Changsha, and Hankou to investigate the production, sales, and export of silk and tea along the Yangtze River. This journey took him seven months and covered five provinces. Along the way, he gained a deep understanding of China's national conditions and people's sentiments. He was especially struck by the desolate scenes from the aftermath of war.

o 图3-10　图为湖北羊楼洞茶场，容
闳曾到此地考察茶业生产

FIRST TRIP TO THE TEA DISTRICTS　91

on the stage of action, Hankau was the most
important entrepôt in China. When the
Taiping rebels captured Woochang in 1856,
Hankau and Han Yang fell at the same time,
and the port was destroyed by fire and was
reduced to ashes. At the time of my visit, the
whole place was rebuilt and trade began to
revive. But the buildings were temporary
shifts. Now the character of the place is completely changed and the foreign residences and
warehouses along the water's edge have given
it altogether a European aspect, so that the
Hankau of today may be regarded as the
Chicago or St. Louis of China, and in no distant
day she is destined to surpass both in trade,
population and wealth. I was in Hankau a few
days before I crossed the Yangtze-Kiang to the
black tea district of Nih Kia Shi.

We left Hankau on the 30th of June and
went over to the tea packing houses in Nih Kia
Shi and Yang Liu Tung on the 4th of July. I
was in those two places over a month and gained
a complete knowledge of the whole process of
preparing the black tea for the foreign market.
The process is very simple and can be easily
learned. I do not know through what preparations the Indian and Assam teas have to

汉口当时尚未通商，惟此事已经提议，不久且实行。

汉口是最重要商埠　当太平军未起事之前，汉口本一中国最重要之商埠。一八五六年，太平军占据武昌时，汉口、汉阳亦同时失陷。以是汉口之一部，尽被焚毁，顿成一片焦土。当予至时，商业已渐恢复，被焚之区，亦从新建筑。第所建房屋，类皆草率急就。若以今日（一九〇九年）之汉口言之，沿岸一带，货栈林立，居屋栉比，类皆壮丽之西式建筑，大有欧西景象，非昔比矣。故在今日中国之有汉口，殆如美国之有芝加哥及圣鲁意二城。予知不久汉口之商业发达，居民繁盛，必将驾芝加哥、圣路易城而上之。予等勾留数日，遂渡扬子江，趋襄家市产墨茶之地。

中国印度茶叶不同　六月三十离汉口，七月四日至杨柳洞（译音）（编者按：应作羊楼洞，在湖北咸宁境内），于此二处，勾留月余。于墨茶之制造及其装运出口之方法，知之甚悉。其法简而易学。予且未知印度茶之制造如何，第以意度之，印茶既以机器制造，其法当亦甚简。自一八五〇年以后，中国人

o 图3-11　左图为容闳回忆录中关于考察汉口的记载，预言汉口未来可比肩美国芝加哥。右图为清人所绘《武昌汉口鸟瞰图》

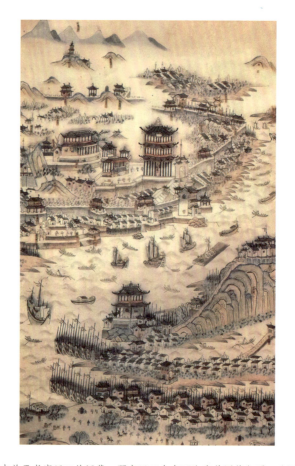

（32）1860年/容闳32岁

太平天国运动已经席卷大半个中国。11月6日，与英国传教士古路吉、杨格非和中国早期留学人曾兰生乘坐"无锡快"小艇，前往太平天国首府天京（今南京）实地考察，拜访已经成为太平天国干王的老友洪仁玕。向洪仁玕提出改造中国的七条建议：一、以科学原则组建一支军队；二、建立军事学校，培养有才干的军官；三、开设水师学堂，建立海军；四、组建文官政府，以有能力有经验的人担任各行政部门的顾问；五、建立银行系统，厘定度量衡标准；六、建立一套适应全民的各级学校教育体系，将《圣经》作为教科书之一；七、设立各种实业学校。表示如"采纳予言，愿为马前走卒"。以农民起义军为班底的太平天国，无法接受这一套超前理论。婉言拒绝洪仁玕的封爵许愿，只收下太平天国护照辞别归沪。

1860/at the age of 32

By November, the Taiping Heavenly Kingdom had swept over half of China. On November 6, Yung Wing and several friends went to the Taiping capital Tian Jing (now Nanjing). He provided Taiping with seven proposals to reform China, covering education, government, and military reform. However, the leaders of the Taiping did not accept his progressive ideas.

o 图3-12　左图为太平天国干王洪仁玕和他撰写的《资政新篇》。这是他向洪秀全提出的一个改革内政和建设国家的新方案，具有鲜明的资本主义色彩。容闳评价他："干王居外久，见识稍广，故较各王略悉外情，即较洪秀全之识见，亦略高一筹。凡欧洲各大强国所以富强之故，亦能知其秘钥所在"。右图为太平天国时期的天京（今南京）

o 图3-13　与容闳一起考察太平天国的英国传教士古路吉、杨格非和中国早期留学人曾兰生（从左到右）

（33）1861年/容闳33岁

出于对太平天国的失望，开始尝试通过积攒财富来实现留学教育计划。利用太平天国护照进出太平天国所辖茶区太平县等采购茶叶，获利不菲。"以予观察所及，太平军之行为，殆无有造新中国之能力，可断言也。于是不得不变计，欲从贸易入手。以为有极巨资财，则借雄厚财力，未必不可图成。"（摘自《西学东渐记》）。

母亲故乡病逝，享年64岁，返回南屏，祭奠亡母，悲恸之中写下"哀哀慈母，生养劬劳，痛绝"。

是年，写组诗《园居十首》，借家乡南屏山村景物抒发情怀："闭门山雨夜，落叶思难禁。"

1861/at the age of 33

Despite his disappointment with the Taipings, Yung Wing still hoped to realize his study abroad plan. Using his Taiping passport, he started building his own savings as a tea agent, purchasing tea from areas under Taiping control, such as Taiping County. However, his mother passed away at the age of 64 in her hometown. Yung Wing returned to Nanping to mourn.

○ 图3-14　19世纪中期江南茶叶贸易图

EXPEDITION TO TAIPING DISTRICT 131

immediately started up to dress myself and quietly woke up the Europeans and Chinese in both boats. As the yelling and whooping drew nearer and nearer it seemed to come from a thousand throats, filling the midnight air with unearthly sounds. In another instant countless torch lights were seen dancing and whirling in the dismal darkness right on the opposite bank. Fortunately the river was between this marauding band and us, while pitch darkness concealed our boats from their sight. In view of such impending danger, we held a council of war. None of us were disposed to fight and endanger our lives in a conflict in which the odds were fearfully against us, there being about a thousand to one. But the English veterinary doctor was the foremost and most strenuous of the Europeans to advocate passive surrender. His countenance actually turned pale and he trembled all over, whether from fear or the chilly atmosphere of the night I could not tell. Having heard from each one what he had to say, I could do nothing but step forward and speak to them, which I did in this wise: "Well, boys, you have all decided not to fight in case we are attacked, but to surrender our treasure. The ground for taking such a step is that we are sure

六英尺，状貌雄伟，望之精神烨然。后乃知此人之心志，亦不坚定，则知人之难也。

予既部署粗定，遂解维趋芜湖。舟中诸人，咸鼓其冒险精神，有陈元龙气概。芜湖山口适中处，有城曰泾县，某日至此而泊。城中驻太平军，其主将曾验予在南京时所得之护照，

明火执仗的数千人

并知予曾识彼中权要者。予舟泊于潮之小湾，小湾面积，适可容数舟。载银二大舟居中，余舟环之。入夜，以枪械分于众人，令皆实子弹。又另增佣金，每人各派一人行夜。分布既毕，始各就寝。就中一年老之茶商及予，睡不成寐。余人因日间劳倦，头着枕，已鼾声动矣。予心既悬悬，不能安寝。卧观天际，见黑云片片，飞行甚速。一弯新月，时从云罅窥人。既而云益浓厚，月不可见，夜色乃益昏沉，黑暗中一无所睹。依枕无聊，长夜将半，耳际忽闻隐隐有呼啸声，由远渐近。乃大惊，披衣起，随各舟人。此时声益近，听之历历可辨，似有数千人，同时呐喊。深夜静野中有此，益觉凄厉。数分钟后，已见对岸火光熊熊，有无数火捻，闪烁于昏黑可怖之世界中。幸此群匪与予舟，尚隔一河。又幸夜黑，予舟尚未为彼所见。

在危险中

予等咸知危险即在目前，向同伴商抵御之策，如临时会议然。咸谓众喜悬殊，果垒者，当以一当千，竟无一人主战。

○ 图3-15　容闳回忆录中关于在太平军所占区域贩茶历险的记载

（34）1862年/容闳34岁

在九江从茶叶经理人转为自营茶行，经营情况虽好，始终心心念念教育计划。

同年，同乡好友唐廷枢编著的《英语集全》出版面世，这是中国现存最早以"英语"命名的汉英字典。

同乡好友黄胜与他人合作编译的《火器略说》出版，主要论述枪炮制造原理。这是近代中国军事现代化的先锋之作。

1862/at the age of 34

As a tea manager in Jiujiang, he switched to running his own tea business and achieved great success.

○ 图3-16　通向九江城门的小巷。容闳曾经经此进出九江

○ 图3-17　《英语集全》及其内页，唐廷枢
编著，其兄唐廷桂、唐廷庚参与校订

（35）1863年/容闳35岁

在九江经营茶叶，接连收到数封上海老友张斯桂、李善兰的安庆来信。信中转述两江总督曾国藩的邀请。

9月，关闭九江茶行，乘船抵达安庆。第二天拜见曾国藩，在回忆录里详细记载了这次会面，并称这一天为登上政治舞台的第一日。对于曾国藩建立枪炮机器厂的想法，容闳向他提出了"制器之器"的建议，即以建立普通基础机械设备为首要，然后通过这些基础机械设备生产制造枪炮、农具、钟表等其他产品的专业机器，并断言"以中国原料之廉，人工之贱，将来自造之机器，必较购之欧美者价廉多矣"。曾国藩采纳了容闳建议，他的日记中也出现了一个新名词："制器之器"。

年底，被授予出洋委员，五品官衔，携款六万八千两白银，前往美国购办机器。协助采购机器者为美国机械工程师约翰·哈斯金。曾国藩幕僚张文虎特作诗《送容闳赴弥利坚采买机器》。

1863/at the age of 35

Yung Wing visited Zeng Guofan, a high ranking official of the imperial court. Yung Wing called this day his first on the political stage. Yung Wing expressed his view that China should construct a machine factory to make machines for the manufacture of arms. Zeng Guofan agreed. Yung Wing was awarded the title of Overseas Commissioner and given 68,000 taels of silver to purchase machinery in America.

○ 图3-18 曾国藩和他在安徽安庆设立的安庆内军械所

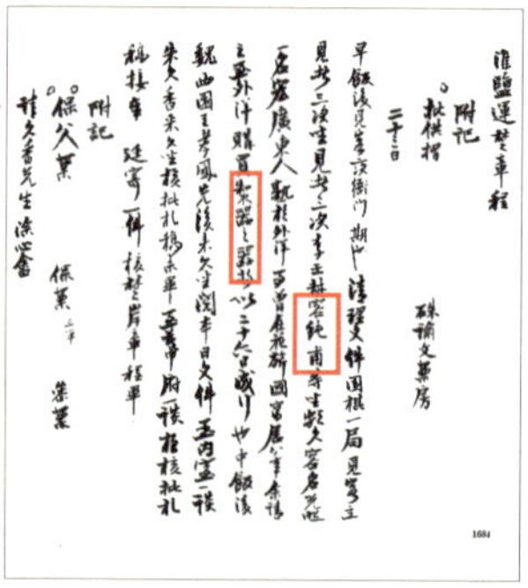

○ 图3-19 接见容闳之后，曾国藩日记中出现了新词“制器之器”：“同治二年十月二十三日 容名光照，一名宏，广东人，熟于外洋事，曾在花旗国寓居八年，余请之至外洋购买制器之器，将以二十六日成行也。”

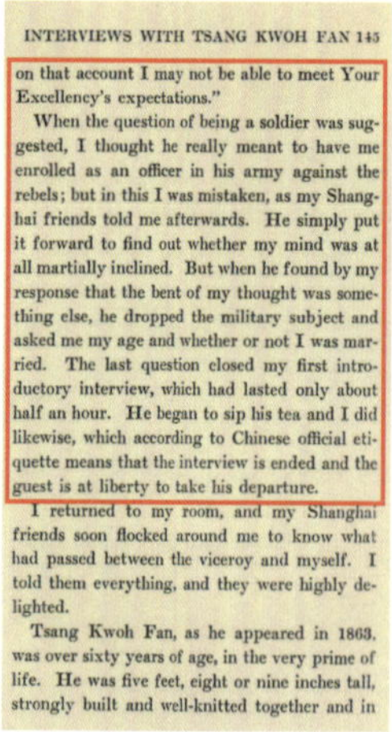

INTERVIEWS WITH TSANG KWOH FAN 145

on that account I may not be able to meet Your Excellency's expectations."

When the question of being a soldier was suggested, I thought he really meant to have me enrolled as an officer in his army against the rebels; but in this I was mistaken, as my Shanghai friends told me afterwards. He simply put it forward to find out whether my mind was at all martially inclined. But when he found by my response that the bent of my thought was something else, he dropped the military subject and asked me my age and whether or not I was married. The last question closed my first introductory interview, which had lasted only about half an hour. He began to sip his tea and I did likewise, which according to Chinese official etiquette means that the interview is ended and the guest is at liberty to take his departure.

I returned to my room, and my Shanghai friends soon flocked around me to know what had passed between the viceroy and myself. I told them everything, and they were highly delighted.

Tsang Kwoh Fan, as he appeared in 1863, was over sixty years of age, in the very prime of life. He was five feet, eight or nine inches tall, strongly built and well-knitted together and in

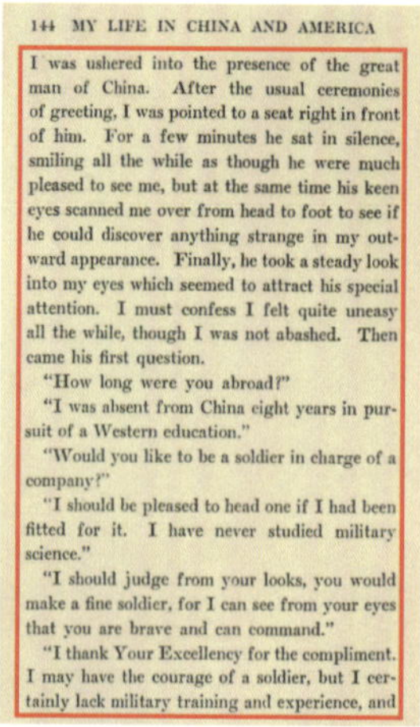

144 MY LIFE IN CHINA AND AMERICA

I was ushered into the presence of the great man of China. After the usual ceremonies of greeting, I was pointed to a seat right in front of him. For a few minutes he sat in silence, smiling all the while as though he were much pleased to see me, but at the same time his keen eyes scanned me over from head to foot to see if he could discover anything strange in my outward appearance. Finally, he took a steady look into my eyes which seemed to attract his special attention. I must confess I felt quite uneasy all the while, though I was not abashed. Then came his first question.

"How long were you abroad?"

"I was absent from China eight years in pursuit of a Western education."

"Would you like to be a soldier in charge of a company?"

"I should be pleased to head one if I had been fitted for it. I have never studied military science."

"I should judge from your looks, you would make a fine soldier, for I can see from your eyes that you are brave and can command."

"I thank Your Excellency for the compliment. I may have the courage of a soldier, but I certainly lack military training and experience, and

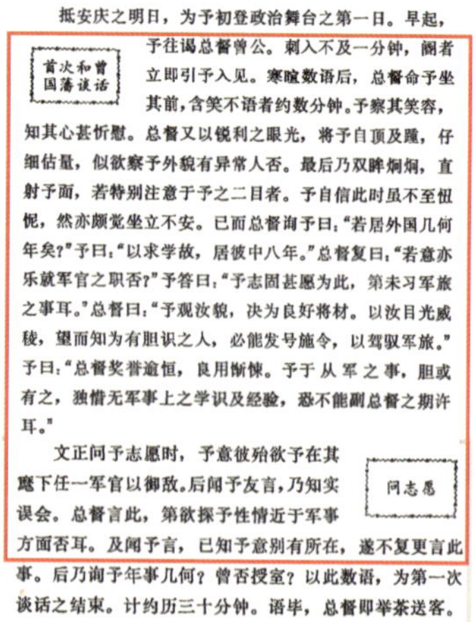

首次和曾国藩谈话

抵安庆之明日，为予初登政治舞台之第一日。早起，予往谒总督曾公。刺入不及一分钟，阍者立即引予入见。寒暄数语后，总督命予坐其前，含笑不语者约数分钟。予察其笑容，知其心甚忻慰。总督又以锐利之眼光，将予自顶及踵，仔细估量，似欲察予外貌有异常人否。最后乃双眸炯炯，直射予面，若特别注意于予之二目者。予自信此时虽不至忸怩，然亦颇觉坐立不安。已而总督询予曰：“若居外国几何年矣？”予曰：“以求学故，居彼中八年。”总督复曰：“若意亦乐就军官之职否？”予答曰：“予志固甚愿为此，第未习军旅之事耳。”总督曰：“予观汝貌，决为良好将材。以汝目光威稜，望而知为有胆识之人，必能发号施令，以驾驭军旅。”予曰：“总督奖誉逾恒，良用惭悚。予于从军之事，胆或有之，独惜无军事上之学识及经验，恐不能副总督之期许耳。”

问志愿

文正问予志愿时，予意彼殆欲予在其麾下任一军官以御敌。后闻予友言，乃知实误会。总督言此，第欲探予性情近于军事方面否耳。及闻予言，已知予意别有所在，遂不复更言此事。后乃询予年事几何？曾否授室？以此数语，为第一次谈话之结束。计约历三十分钟。语毕，总督即举茶送客。

○ 图3-20 容闳回忆录中关于拜见曾国藩的记载

（36）1864年/容闳36岁

赴美采购机器，途经开罗、亚历山大和法国南方第一大港马赛，游历巴黎和伦敦世界都会，大开眼界，对欧洲工业革命带来的社会经济变革有了更直接、更深刻的了解。

初春，到达美国，与位于马萨诸塞州的朴得南公司签署订购机器合同。

"十年前以优异成绩毕业于耶鲁大学的中国学生容闳，作为中国政府的代理人，以清国官吏的身份来到美国，购买各种机器引进中国。天朝的人希望借此能够师夷长技。"（摘自美国《特拉华公报》）

7月，到纽黑文参加耶鲁大学同学毕业十周年聚会。"旧雨重逢，一堂聚话，人人兴高采烈，欢乐异常。虽自毕业分袂后，十载于兹，而诸同学之感情，仍不减当年亲密。予乃有缘得躬与其盛，何幸如之。"（摘自《西学东渐记》）。

安排侄子容尚勤入读母校孟松学校，珠海南屏容氏由此成为近代中国最早出现第二代留学人的家族。

1864/at the age of 36

Yung Wing traveled to America to purchase machinery. *The Delaware Gazette* writes about his visit, "Ten years ago, Yung Wing, a Chinese student graduated with honors from Yale University. He has now come as an agent of the Chinese government to purchase various machines for importation to China. The people of the Celestial Empire hope to learn from the Westerners and improve their skills." In July, he attended his ten-year reunion with his Yale classmates in New Haven.

○ 图3-21　采购机器回国前，在康州哈特福德镇留影，左为容闳亲笔手迹。

○ 图3-22　采购机器期间与美国同学合影（右一）为容闳

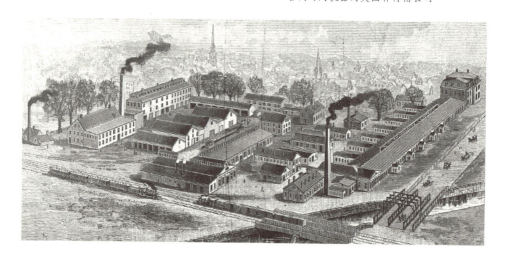

○ 图3-23　左图为美国《特拉华公报》8月26日关于容闳来美采买机器的报道。下图为容闳订购机器的美国朴得南公司

（37）/容闳37岁

8月，在美国订制的上百种新式机器顺利运达上海。以这批世界一流的机器为主，建成了中国第一个机器制造厂，即闻名遐迩的江南机器制造总局，开启了中国近代民族工业的先河。直到20世纪初期这里仍然是亚洲最大的机器制造厂。

9月，赴徐州向曾国藩述职。已升任两江总督的曾国藩，对于容闳不辱使命极为赞许，向朝廷专折请奖，称赞容闳此行"不避险阻，涉历重洋，为时逾两年之久，计程越四万里而遥，实与古人出使绝域，其难相当，应予奖励"。

10月，获得朝廷候补同知五品官衔，在江苏巡抚署担任翻译。

1865/at the age of 37

In August, over a hundred of the new machines that Yung Wing had ordered from the United States arrived in Shanghai. With these machines, China's first machine factory, called the Jiangnan Arsenal, was established, Through the beginning of the 20th century, the Jiangnan Arsenal remained the largest machine manufacturing plant in Asia. In October, Yung Wing was promoted as a translator in the administrative office of Jiangsu.

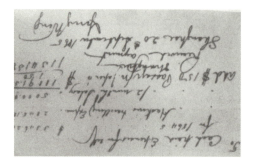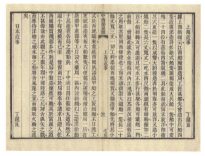

o 图3-24　容闳手书采购机器支销单和《中西闻见录》之"上海近事"关于容闳采购机器的记载

o 图3-25　江南制造总局造炮车间

o 图3-26　江南创造总局的工人们正在锻造炮管

（38）1866年/容闳38岁

随两淮盐运使丁日昌居扬州半年，二人交往深厚。"丁为一具有进步倾向之人，且勇于实行一切改革之措施。"（摘自《西学东渐记》）其间翻译科尔顿《地理学》与帕森《契约论》等西方著作，协助丁日昌协调江南制造总局工作；是年，曾国藩在给丁日昌的信函中，赞誉容闳为"中国可造之才"。

是年，孙中山在距离容闳故乡南屏三十多公里的翠亨村出生。

1866/at the age of 38

During his six-month stay in Yangzhou, Yung Wing developed a close relationship with Ding Richang, Jiangsu's Salt Transport Commissioner. He translated Western works such as Colton's *Geography* and *The Social Contract*.

It is said that Parsons' Law of Contracts has received the distinction of being translated into Chinese, the translation being done by Yung Wing, the Chinese Commissioner of Education in this country.

386 THE NEW JERSEY LAW JOURNAL.

That we request, as a last and fitting tribute of respect to the memory of our deceased brother, that the Courts of the County do now adjourn, and that these resolutions be ordered to be entered on the minutes thereof.

That a copy of these resolutions be transmitted to the family of the deceased.

CHARLES M. JESSUP, died at his residence in Newark, September 18th, in the 28th year of his age. Mr. Jessup, for one so young in years, had won for himself a prominent place in the chosen profession of his life, having occupied the position of Police Justice of the city for several years, whose duties he discharged with marked intelligence and fidelity. A meeting of the Bar was held on the 20th instant, in the Common Pleas court room, and the following preamble and resolutions were unanimously adopted :

WHEREAS, The hand of death has again entered into the ranks of our profession and taken from us one of the most genial and promising members thereof :

Resolved, That the bar of Essex county learn with deep regret of the death of Charles M. Jessup, Esq., young in years, stricken in the very morning of life, manly, courteous and gentlemanly in character, we cheerfully bear testimony to his true friendship, his legal ability, and very promising professional usefulness.

Resolved, That we extend our cordial sympathy to the family of the deceased.

Resolved, That the Circuit Court be requested to direct these resolutions to be entered on the minutes of the court.

Resolved, That the members of the court attend the funeral of our deceased brother in a body.

Resolved, That a copy of these resolutions be sent to the family of the deceased and published in the daily papers.

GENERALITIES.

It is said that Parsons' Law of Contracts has received the distinction of being translated into Chinese, the translation being done by Yung Wing, the Chinese Commissioner of Education in this country.

In order to prevent, as far as possible, the evils which arise from the parade of difference of opinion in the court of last resort, the Supreme Court of Michigan has decided, that in cases where the court is equally divided, the members of the court will deliver no opinions, but simply affirm the judgment below.

Judge Keogh, the Irish judge who, while insane, attempted to kill his servant the other day, is the judge who tried the celebrated election case at Galway, in 1872, by which the priests' candidate was unseated on the ground of intimidation—the priests having threatened to excommunicate all who should vote against their candidate—and forty-two priests and two bishops were suspended from the exercise of the franchise for seven years. The indignation thus stirred up against Judge Keogh, who is a Roman Catholic, was most intense. When he went upon his circuit, he was constantly protected by military or constabulary forces which accompanied him. Perhaps the intense strain to which he has been subjected has had much to do with his reported insanity.

MISCELLANEOUS.

A case which has excited considerable comment, and no little amusement, is the now famous suit for a penny. A certain Mr. Watson, traveling on the Metropolitan (underground) Railroad, neglected to provide himself with a ticket, but tendered the fare, seven pence, on reaching his destination. This the railroad official refused to accept, on the ground that the company charged an extra penny for not having procured a ticket. This Mr. Watson refused to pay, denying the right of a railroad company to impose fines upon its customers—the traveling public—and the company brought suit to recover. Mr. Watson's course was sustained, and the company appealed. They have already been beaten twice, and the "suit for a penny" is now before the Court of Appeals. If, as is expected, this court sustains Mr. Watson, the case will be taken before the House of Lords, when we may hope it will be definitely set at rest.—San Francisco Post.

IMPORTANT DECISIONS ELSEWHERE

Action by Surgeon.—Evidence. 1. In an action for a surgeon's fee, where the value of the services is denied, and a counterclaim for damages for malpractice is set up, it is proper for the court to instruct the jury, as a matter of law, that the plaintiff was a competent surgeon. 2. Where the value of the service is denied, and a counterclaim is set up, the presumption is that the plaintiff's treatment of the case was skillful, and "that he was competent for the task which he had undertaken, and did his duty to the best of his

○图3-27 美国《新泽西法律专刊》报道容闳翻译《契约论》的消息，报道称"《契约论》已经很荣幸地被容闳翻译成中文"

○图3-28 晚清洋务大员、容闳的良师益友丁日昌

（39）1867年/容闳39岁

陪同曾国藩考察江南制造总局，借机提出在制造局附属设立一座兵工学校，培养中国青年学习机械工程的理论和操作，曾国藩深为赞许。

6月，针对中国航运完全被外国商轮垄断，在上海发起筹组华商轮船公司，草拟《联设轮船公司章程》，这是中国第一个民营公司组建方案。此举得到曾国藩大力支持，并专门上奏清廷。5年后，李鸿章创建轮船招商局，这份章程成为重要参考文件，容闳好友唐廷枢（今珠海唐家湾人）和徐润（今珠海北岭村人）出任总办和会办。

是年，经曾国藩举荐，容闳"以同知留于江苏"。

1867/at the age of 39

Yung Wing proposed to Zeng Guofan the establishment of a military school affiliated with the manufacturing bureau. The idea was to train Chinese students in theoretical and practical mechanical engineering. Zeng Guofan deeply appreciated the idea. In June, Yung Wing proposed that China establish a wholly owned Chinese steamship company. The idea was accepted. Yung Wing drafted the "Articles of Association for the Joint Establishment of Steamship Companies, "marking the first plan for the formation of a private company in China.

○ 图3-29　图为曾国藩奏陈容闳的《联设新轮船公司章程》

In 1867, Viceroy Tsang Kwoh Fan, with Li Hung Chang's co-operation, succeeded in ending the Nienfi rebellion, and came to Nanking to fill his viceroyalty of the two Kiangs.

Before taking up his position as viceroy of the Kiangs permanently, he took a tour of inspection through his jurisdiction and one of the important places he visited was Shanghai and the Kiang Nan Arsenal—an establishment of his own creation. He went through the arsenal with undisguised interest. I pointed out to him the machinery which I bought for him in America. He stood and watched its automatic movement with unabated delight, for this was the first time he had seen machinery, and how it worked. It was during this visit that I succeeded in persuading him to have a mechanical school annexed to the arsenal, in which Chinese youths might be taught the theory as well as the practice of mechanical engineering, and thus enable China in time to dispense with the employment of foreign mechanical engineers and machinists, and to be perfectly independent. This at once appealed to the practical turn of the Chinese mind, and the school was finally added to the arsenal. They are doubtless turning out at the present time both mechanical engineers and machinists of all descriptions.

亦恐销路不广，因在中国法庭中，因据约而兴讼论者很少；聊或有之，而违背契约之案件，亦自有中国法律可据，与国之法律，实不合于中国情势云。一八六七年，文正得举文忠襄助，平定挂捻，乃至南京就任两江总督，未抵任前，先于所辖境内巡行一周，以视察民情风俗。而其往者，则其亲创之江南制造局也。文正来亲视察此局，似觉有非常兴趣。予知其于机器为创制，因导其历览由美购回各物，并试验自行运动之机，明示以应用之方法。文正见之大乐，予遂乘此机会，复劝其于厂旁立一兵工学校，招中国学生肆业其中，探讨机器工程上之理论与实验，以期中国将来不必需用外国机械及外国工程师，文正极赞许，不久遂遂实行。今日制造局之兵工学校，已遂就无数机械工程师矣。

第十六章　予之教育计划

予自得谒于曾文正，于江南制造局内附设兵工学校，向所怀教育计划，可谓小试其锋，既略表我怀，曾文正者，固者无知己之感，则其赏识勉励者，遂联欢联款试。曾文正者，予余有知己之感，今日政界不重要人，则与余志同道合者，又有老友丁日昌。丁为人有血气，好任事，

○ 图3-30　容闳回忆录中关于陪同曾国藩考察江南制造局提议建立兵工学校的记载

○ 图3-31　图为轮船招商局成立庆典

（40）1868年/容闳40岁

向升任江苏巡抚的丁日昌正式提出留学教育计划，拟就"条陈四则"，由丁日昌递交军机大臣文祥，代为上奏朝廷。主要内容是：一、组织合资汽船公司，纯粹华人参股，不允许外国资本进入。二、选派颖秀青年出洋留学，以为国家储蓄人才。派遣之法，初次可先定120名学额以试行之，又分为四批，按年递派，每年派送30人，留学期限定为十五年。三、设法开采矿产以尽地利。四、禁止教会干涉民间诉讼，以防外力之侵入。"此条陈之第一、三、四，特假以陪衬，眼光所注而望其必成者，自在第二条。"（摘自《西学东渐记》）。可惜文祥因母亲去世返家居丧，计划搁浅，"予目的怀之十年，不得一试。才见萌蘖，遽遭严霜，亦安能无怏怏哉。……自一八六八年至一八七〇年，此三年中，无日不悬悬然不得要领"。（摘自《西学东渐记》）

2月，清廷聘请卸任美国驻华公使蒲安臣代表朝廷率队出访美国。这是中国政府向欧美派出的第一个外交使团。双方签订《中美续增条约》，承诺中国人到美国学习可获得优惠待遇。这成为中国派遣学生留学美国的法律依据。

容闳好友邝其照在香港出版《字典集成》，这是第一本由中国人编写的英语字典。

与徐润、徐荣村、潘爵臣、李贯之等五名广东商人各出资五千两白银开设"通源杂粮土号"，经营茶叶出口。

1868/at the age of 40

Presented his study abroad plan to Ding Richang, proposing "...to send picked Chinese youths abroad to be thoroughly educated for the public service." Unfortunately, the plan was ignored.

In February, the Qing court hired Anson Burlingame, the former American minister to China, to lead a delegation to visit Europe and America. As a result of that tour, the "Burlingame Treaty" was signed. This became China's legal basis for sending students to study in the United States and for Yung Wing's realization of his dream.

o 图3-32　左图为卸任美国驻华公使蒲安臣。右图为蒲安臣使团拜见美国总统约翰逊

（41）1869年/容闳41岁

向曾国藩倡议建立的江南制造总局附属兵工学校江南制造局翻译馆破土动工。与好友徐寿、华蘅芳等，为江南制造总局翻译馆制定了《再拟开办学馆事宜章程十六条》，其中之一就是招收学生，培养翻译科技书刊的专门人才和技术人才。后来，江南制造总局翻译馆翻译西方科学著作近160种，成为晚清中国译书最多、影响最大的科技编译机构。

经徐润介绍，与苏州女郑氏在上海成婚。住上海天同路唐家弄43弄6号。无子嗣。《容氏谱牒》记载为"副郑氏"。后离异。

1869/at the age of 41

The groundbreaking ceremony for the affiliated Military Industry School of the Jiangnan Arsenal, proposed to Zeng Guofan by Yung Wing. Later, the Translation Office of the Jiangnan Arsenal developed into the largest and most influential institution for the translation of scientific and technological works in the late Qing.

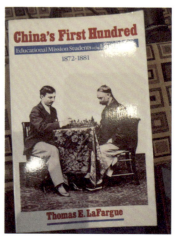

○ 图3-33　5月5日容闳与恩师布朗的长子罗伯特·马礼逊·布朗在上海下棋（左）。后来，该图片成为最早系统研究留美幼童教育的专著*China First Hundred 1872-1881*的封面图（右）

○ 图3-34　　左图为和容闳一起制定《再拟开办学馆事宜章程十六条》的徐寿（右）、华蘅芳（左）在江南制造总局翻译馆留影。右图为江南制造局翻译馆

第四章　留美幼童

(1870—1881)

The Chinese Educational Mission "CEM"

（42）1870年/容闳42岁

　　作为译员参与曾国藩、丁日昌等朝廷重臣处理震惊中外的"天津教案"。当时，数十名外国传教士和中国信徒被杀，教堂被焚烧、英、美、俄、普、比、西七国联合向清政府抗议。英国周刊《伦敦和中国电讯》报道了容闳随丁日昌赴天津协助办理教案的消息，报道称："容闳留学美国多年，毕业于耶鲁大学。丁日昌认为，容闳的这种经历及其形成的思想观念，有助于处理类似天津教案这样的涉外危机。"文章还报道了曾国藩在天津向容闳等详细了解西方国家军事、经济等方面的情况。借此机会，容闳再次向丁日昌提出留学教育计划，力陈开启民智刻不容缓，引起了曾国藩、李鸿章等重臣的共鸣，并决定摘取容闳所写出洋留学条陈联衔上奏清廷。容闳闻讯倍感欣慰。"予对故土及同胞之爱长盛不衰，并因恻隐之心与日俱增。予苦心孤诣以竟派遣幼童留美之事，此洵为予对华夏永恒热爱之举，亦予以为维新复兴中华最切实可行之策。"（摘自《西学东渐记》）

1870/at age of 42

　　As a translator, Yung Wing participated in the handling of the "Tianjin Missionary Case" that shocked China and foreign countries. The British magazine *London and China Telegraph* reported on Yung Wing's assistance in handling the case in Tianjin with Ding Richang. Yung Wing asked Ding Richang to again propose his study abroad program to the commissioners. This time, the proposal was accepted.

o 图4-1 左图为1869年落成的
天津望海楼教堂，次年成为天
津教案的发生地。右为熊熊燃
烧的望海楼教堂

We have been told that Ting Futai took with him to Tientsin a Chinese gentleman named Yung Wing, who had travelled and studied in America, and is, in fact, a graduate of Yale College, and another Chinese, who was recently interpreter at the French Consulate at Shanghai, and who travelled and studied in Europe. Ting naturally considered that their knowledge of foreign character and ideas would be useful in dealing with such a crisis as that of Tientsin. And soon after their arrival they were summoned into the presence of Tseng-kwo-Fan, who questioned them long and earnestly as to the military resources and wealth of western nations. He asked the interpreter more especially about France. Finally he asked him which of *all* western nations was, in his opinion, the most powerful. The unwary linguist answered, France. " Why ?"

o 图4-2 1870年12月5日，英国周刊《伦敦和中国电讯》报道了容闳随丁日昌赴天津协助办理教案的消息

第十七章　经理留学事务所
（派送第一批留学生）

曾等四人联名入奏

钦派四大臣中，曾文正实为领袖。当诸人未散时，予乃乘机进言于丁抚，请其向曾督重提教育事，并商诸其他二人。予知丁于三年前已向曾督及此，故曾当已略知此中梗概，丁又素表同情于予，得此二公力助，馀二人当无不赞成矣。一夕，丁抚归甚晚，予已寝。丁就予室，呼予起，谓此事已得曾公同意，将四人联衔入奏，请政府采择君所条陈而实行之。予闻此消息，乃喜而不寐，竟夜开眼如夜鹰，觉此身飘飘然如凌云步虚，忘其为僵卧床第间。两日后，奏折拜发，文正领衔，馀三人皆署名，由驿站加紧快骑，飞递入京，此

90

o 图4-3 容闳回忆录中记载了当时听到自己出洋留学条陈即将被上奏朝廷的消息时欣喜若狂的心情

（43）1871年/容闳43岁

前往南京，曾国藩接到"着照所请"的朱批，急邀容闳火速前往商定派遣学生出洋事宜，酝酿成立预备学校，制定留学章程。"至此予之教育计划，方成为确有之事实，将于中国两千年历史中特开新纪元矣。"（摘自《西学东渐记》）

9月3日，曾国藩李鸿章联名呈上《拟选聪颖子弟前赴泰西各国肄习技艺以培人才折》称："选聪颖幼童。送赴泰西各国书院学习军政、船政，步算、制造诸学。约计十年余业成而归，使西人擅长之技，中国皆能谙熟，然后可以渐图自强。"

9月9日，清廷批准奏折。同年，清政府在上海成立"幼童出洋肄业局沪局"，挑选学生进入"预备学校"，受命主持招生事宜。

因报名学生极少，亲赴香港英文学校和得风气之先的家乡招生，首批30学生名额得以完成，这批学生中24人为广东籍贯，其中5名为今珠海籍。回乡期间，为父母迁坟合葬于橘树山上。捐银五百两，在南屏创建甄贤社学，后邀请清末学者、香港《华字日报》主笔王韬撰写 《征设香山南屏乡义学序》。

1871/at the age of 43

On September 9, the Qing court approved the memorial. That same year, the Qing court established "The Chinese Educational Commission.（CEM）Yung Wing was put in charge of enrollment and selected students to enter a "Preparatory School" for preparing students to go overseas.

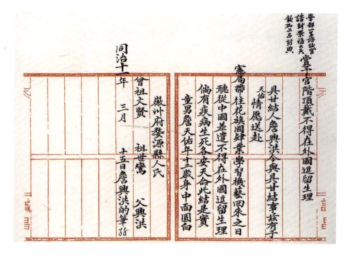

○ 图4-4 图为詹天佑父亲签署的具结书，承诺"倘有疾病生死，各安天命"

○ 图4-5 图为詹天佑的父亲詹兴洪、母亲陈氏和詹天佑的三女儿合影

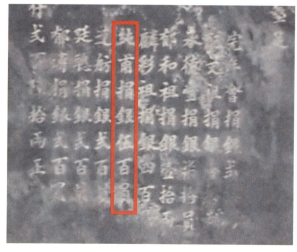

○ 图4-6 图为珠海甄贤社学碑刻上记录容闳捐银办学五百两

（44）1872年/容闳44岁

正月十九日，曾国藩、李鸿章再次联衔上奏《遴派委员携带幼童出洋肄业兼陈应办事宜恭折》，认为"挑选幼童出洋肄业固属中华创始之举，抑亦古来未有之事"，建议派遣"容闳为副委员，常驻美国，经理一切事宜"。

3月12日，曾国藩于南京去世。容闳深为曾国藩未能看到其开创的事业开花结果而痛惜。"设天假以年，使文正更增一龄者，则第一批学生已出洋，犹得见其手植桃李，欣欣向荣。"（摘自《西学东渐记》）

7月，先行赴美，为留美幼童做安置准备。与康州教育局官员诺斯洛普先生商议将幼童分散寄宿到美国家庭中，便于他们尽快熟悉语言。此举得到当地民众的支持。据统计，120名留美幼童最后分散到新英格兰地区的54个家庭中，其中康涅狄格州34户，马萨诸塞州20户。

8月11日，第一批30名留美幼童乘坐美国邮轮"共和号"从上海吴淞口启程赴美，开启了他们参与中国近代社会变革的破冰之旅。蔡绍基、张康仁、容尚谦、邓士聪、谭耀勋等五名珠海幼童名列其中。

9月22日，幼童抵达目的地马萨诸塞州春田城，这一天后来被马萨诸塞州确定为"容闳和中国留美幼童纪念日"。

1872/at the age of 44

Zeng Guofan and Li Hongzhang jointly submitted a memorial to the imperial court. They suggested dispatching "Yung Wing as vice commissioner, stationed in the United States, to manage all matters." In July, Yung Wing arrived in the United States and made preparations for the CEM. He would place the 120 CEM students in the homes of 54 local families. In September, the first group of CEM arrived in America.

○ 图4-7 曾国藩和李鸿章的《遴派委员携带幼童出洋肄业兼陈应办事宜恭折》

○ 图4-8 1872年2月，容闳写信给自己当年老师、时任耶鲁大学校长波特，详细介绍了留美幼童计划和当时准备工作的进展，恳请老师和耶鲁大学的教授们探讨"适合于将这些孩子们培养成为最为有用的人才的最佳教育模式"。图为波特校长（左）和容闳写给他的信（右）

ID#	Name	姓名	Anglicized Name	Place	Host Family
1	Cai Jinzhang	蔡錦章	Tsoy Cum Ching	Washington, Conn.	Mrs. Jedediah (Julia Leavitt) Richards
2	Cai Shaoji	蔡紹基	Tsai Shou Kie	Hartford, Conn.	David E. and Fannie P. (Hinsdale) Bartlett
3	Cao Jifu	曹吉福			
4	Chen Jurong	陳距溶	Chin [Chun] Kee Yung	Granby, Conn.	Rev. Thomas D. and Amelia (Castle) Murphy
5	Chen Ronggui	陳榮貴	Chun [Chin] Yung Kwei		
6	Cheng Daqi	程大器	Tsing Ta Chi		
7	Deng Shicong	鄧士聰	Tyng Se Chung	Granby, Conn.	Rev. Thomas D. and Amelia (Castle) Murphy
8	He Tingliang	何廷樑	Ho Ting Liang	Northampton, Mass.	[Miss Martha Ely Matthews]?
9	Huang Kaijia	黃開甲	Wong Kae [Kai] Kah	Hartford, Conn.	David E. and Fannie P. (Hinsdale) Bartlett
10	Huang Xibao	黃錫寶	Wong Set Pow		
11	Huang Zhongliang	黃仲良	Wong Chung Liang	Wilbraham, Mass.?	
12	Kuang Rongguang	鄺榮光	Kwong Yung Kwang	Northampton, Mass.?	[Miss Martha Ely Matthews]?
13	Liang Dunyan	梁敦彥	Liang Tun Yen	Hartford, Conn.	David E. and Fannie P. (Hinsdale) Bartlett
14	Liu Jiazhao	劉家照	Low [Lew] Kia Chau	Oakham, Mass.	Miss Martha E. Burt
15	Lu Yongquan	陸永泉	Chuan Lok Wing	Washington, Conn.	Mrs. Jedediah (Julia Leavitt) Richards
16	Luo Guorui	羅國瑞	Loh Kwok Shui	Bridgeport, Conn.	Rev. Guy B. and Mary (Barnes) Day
17	Niu Shangzhou	牛尚周	Niu Shung Chow	Springfield, Mass.	Henry R. and Sarah W. (Lewis) Vaille
18	Ouyang Geng	歐陽庚	Owyang Keng	Bridgeport, Conn.	Rev. Guy B. and Mary (Barnes) Day
19	Pan Mingzhong	潘銘鍾	Pawn Wing Chung	West Haven, Conn.	Luther H. and Martha J. Northrop
20	Qian Wenkui	錢文魁	Chieng Wan Kwei		
21	Rong Shangqian	容尚謙	Yung Shang Him	Springfield, Mass.	Alexander S. and Rebekah R. (Brown) McClean
22	Shi Jintang	石錦堂	Zah Ching Dong		
23	Shi Jinyong	史錦鏞	Shih Chin Yung		
24	Tan Yaoxun	譚耀勛	Tan Yew Fun	Oakham, Mass.	Miss Martha E. Burt
25	Wu Yangzeng	吳仰曾	Woo Yang Tsang	Hartford, Conn.	David E. and Fannie P. (Hinsdale) Bartlett
26	Zeng Dugong	曾篤恭	Spencer Laisun	**	**
27	Zhan Tianyou	詹天佑	Jeme Tien Yow	West Haven, Conn.	Luther H. and Martha J. Northrop
28	Zhang Kangren	張康仁	Chang Hong Yen	Bridgeport, Conn.	[Rev. Guy B. and Mary (Barnes) Day]?
29	Zhong Juncheng	鍾俊成	Chung Tsung Ching	Wilbraham, Mass.?	
30	Zhong Wenyao	鍾文耀	Chung Mun Yew	Springfield, Mass.	Alexander S. and Rebekah R. (Brown) McClean

○ 图4-9 图为第一批留美幼童寄宿家庭安置一览表

○ 图4-10　第一批留美幼童抵达合影。左图（从左向右）依次为钟文耀、梁敦彦、黄仲良、史锦镛、蔡绍基、牛尚周旧金山时合影，右图（从左向右）依次为邝荣光、张康仁、唐国安、何廷梁、苏锐钊、邝景垣

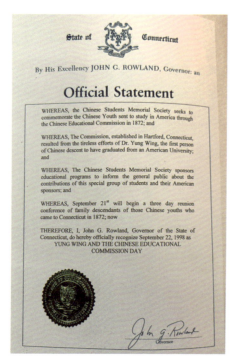

○ 图4-11 左图为马萨诸塞州把幼童抵达的9月22日确定为"容闳和中国留美幼童纪念日"的文件。下图为首批留美幼童乘坐的美国邮轮"共和号",建于1866年

（45）1873年/容闳45岁

6月，第二批幼童30名抵达美国。黄有章、容尚勤、唐元湛、梁金荣、邓桂廷、张有恭、蔡廷干、唐国安、卓仁志等九名珠海幼童名列其中。领队为容闳好友、珠海东岸村人黄胜和新会人容增祥。安置幼童后返回天津，带回中国第一台新式武器格林炮，一个月后订购50尊，后陆续增订。"予甚愿中国有最新式之军械，犹望中国有新学问之人才也。"（摘自《西学东渐记》）

陪同李鸿章与秘鲁特使葛尔西耶就派遣华工问题谈判，曾在澳门多次目睹被贩卖华工"以辫相连，结成一串，牵往囚室"的惨状，力阻与秘鲁签约。

与时任轮船招商局总办唐廷枢（今珠海唐家湾人）、时任上海知县叶廷眷（今珠海吉大人）以及郑观应一起，在上海筹办《汇报》，容闳从美国亲自购置机器和铅字。次年，《汇报》正式创刊，成为上海第一份中国人创办的中文报刊。

1873/at the age of 45

In June, the second group of 30 CEM students arrived. After settling the children, Yung Wing returned to Tianjin and brought back the first modern weapon to China-the Gatling gun. He accompanied Li Hongzhang to discuss the issue of the importation of coolie labor to Peru with Garcia Jérez, the Peruvian envoy. Along with friends he helped set up the *Huibao in* Shanghai, the city's first native owned modern Chinese-language daily newspaper.

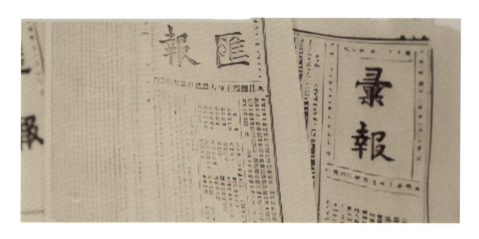

○ 图4-12　容闳参与创办的《汇报》。据《申报》报道："现闻粤人拟在上海另开新闻馆一所，首先倡捐者，上海令叶邑侯也，倡议开馆者，唐君景星诸人也，倡立馆规者，容君纯甫也，主笔诸君，皆延请粤中名宿也。机器铅字，皆容君所承办也。""叶邑侯"即叶廷眷，"唐君景星"即唐廷枢，"容君纯甫"即容闳。《汇报》后易名《彙报》《益报》

○ 图4-13　1872年的格林炮式样

（46）1874年/容闳46岁

9月，第三批幼童30名抵达美国，唐绍仪、徐振鹏、唐致尧、梁如浩、容星桥等五名珠海幼童名列其中。

是年，奉李鸿章指令，赴秘鲁秘密调查华工受虐之事，这是清政府第一次调查海外华工状况的活动。当地媒体报道了容闳的秘鲁之行，容闳挚友吐依曲尔牧师、妻兄威廉·凯洛克博士陪同前往。容闳现场拍摄了24张照片，显示"华工背部受笞被烙斑斑之伤痕"惨状。他在给清廷总理衙门的报告中说："华工到彼，被卖开山种蔗及（在）糖寮、鸟粪岛（工作），（备受）虐待。合同限内，打死及自尽，投火炉、糖锅，死者甚多，实可惨悯。"图文并茂的调查报告，为李鸿章在《中秘友好通商条约》换约谈判中坚持对华工的保护发挥了重要作用。容闳成为"我国运用摄影图片进行对外交涉的第一个外交官"。

9月，留美幼童容尚勤（今珠海南屏人）、曾溥考入耶鲁大学，是最早考入大学的留美幼童。

1874/at the age of 46

Yung wing was ordered by Li Hongzhang to secretly investigate the situation of Chinese workers in Peru. This was the first investigation of overseas Chinese workers conducted by the Qing court. Yung Wing personally took 24 photos to document the tragic situation of Chinese workers. The illustrated investigative report provided strong evidence for Li Hongzhang's negotiations with Peru. Yung Wing became the first diplomat in China to use photographic images for foreign negotiations.

○ 图4-14 1874年容闳等赴秘鲁调查华工
受虐情况的船票，船票背面有容闳手迹

THE Chinese Commissioner, who has been for many months in Cuba and the United States enquiring into the treatment of the Chinese coolies, has arrived in this port, and will, we believe, make prolix investigations into the condition and prospects of his fellow countrymen in this country. He is accompanied by two American gentlemen, both of whom, we believe, hold appointments from the Chinese Government.

○ 图4-15　图为陪同容闳赴秘鲁调查
的挚友吐依曲尔牧师和他收集的关于
容闳赴秘鲁调查的英文报道，报道称
中国专员（容闳）已经抵达（秘鲁）
港口，他将对他的手足同胞在秘鲁的
生活工作状况进行调查，他有两位美
国绅士陪同

布片于众。所以不能全部体现出"新闻照片"的特点，严格说来，只是一种规定时间内的纪念摄影。

在纪实摄影活动中容闳是一位杰出的代表。容闳(1828——1912)字纯甫，广东香山县人，清末改良主义者。1847年留学美国，1854年毕业于耶鲁大学，是我国在美国高等学府毕业的第一人。1885年回国，为江南制造局采购外国机器。1870年与陈兰彬分任留学生正、副监督。后兼任驻美国、秘鲁副使。老年客居美国。

图28　容闳（1828—1912），我国运用摄影图片进行对外交涉的第一个外交官。

容闳久居国外，眼界开扩，并会摄影。在办理华工条约交涉中，出色地把摄影用于外交事务，维护了侨胞的权益。同治十二年（1873）秘鲁派专使来华，拟与中国签定招募华工条约。在此之前，秘鲁已有大批华工，受到非人待遇，中国政府早有所闻。但又无实据来回绝秘鲁。于是经办此事的李鸿章就委派容闳去秘鲁调查当地华工的处境，以决定可否签约。容闳到秘鲁后"以迅速之手段，三阅月内即调查完竣"。随后容闳将报告书及亲手拍摄的24幅照片一并封寄国内，这份报告书和24幅照片是华工在秘鲁受到虐待与歧视的真实写照。并写信嘱咐先不出示此据。容闳在他的回忆录中叙述了这24幅照片的拍摄过程："凡华工背部受笞，被略斑斑之伤痕者，令人不忍目睹者，予乃借以摄影，一一呈现于世人目中。予摄此影，皆于夜中秘密为之，除此身受其虐之数华工外，无一人知之者。此数名之华工，亦由予密告为故，私约之来也。秘鲁华工之工场，直一牲畜场。场中种种野蛮之举动，残暴无复人理，摄影特其一斑耳。有此确凿证据，无论口若悬河，当亦无辩护之余地"。[3]

容闳站在祖国和民族的立场上，以摄影作为揭露罪恶，主持正义

· 56 ·

o 图4-16　上图为《中国摄影史1840—1937》（中国摄影出版社出版1987年8月第一版）关于容闳秘鲁摄影的记载，称之为中国纪实摄影第一人。下图为容闳秘鲁所拍照片

o 图4-17 图为容闳秘鲁所拍照片

（47）1875年/容闳47岁

3月，容闳和留美幼童寄居家庭的康州姑娘玛丽·路易莎·凯洛克小姐举行婚礼，当地的媒体进行了报道。

11月，第四批幼童30名抵达，唐荣浩、唐荣俊、盛文扬、吴其藻、谭耀芳等五名珠海幼童名列其中，领队为幼童预备学校教习、中国首部英汉词典编撰者邝其照。第四批幼童启程前在上海轮船招商总局门前合影。至此，由容闳倡导并促成的中国首次官派120名留美幼童全部派遣完毕，120名幼童中，84名来自广东，其中39名来自香山，属于今珠海的24人。另外同行还有10名自费留美幼童，其中半数以上出自今珠海，他们是世博会中国首名金奖获得者徐荣村以及徐润、黄胜后人。

12月，被任命为驻美国、西班牙、秘鲁副公使兼幼童出洋肄业局副监督，官居二品顶戴候补道台。

1875/at the age of 47

In March, Yung Wing married Mary Kellogg. In November, the final fourth group of 30 CEM students arrived. Of the 120 CEM students, 24 were from Zhuhai, Yung Wing's hometown. In December, Yung Wing was appointed as the Associate Minister to the United States, Spain and Peru, as well as the Associate Commissioner of "The Chinese Educational Commission."

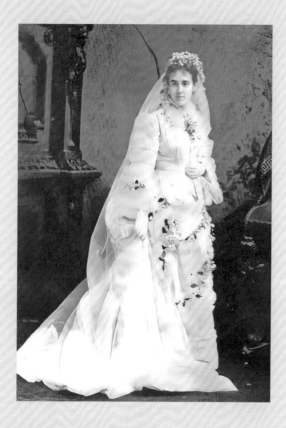

○图4-18 容闳妻子婚纱照

vision, and a new writ was ordered to be issued for the county of Tipperary.

YUNG WING MARRIES A CONNECTICUT LADY.—Mr. Yung Wing, of Canton, China, chief of the Chinese Educational Commission, now at Hartford, was married on Wednesday to Miss Mary L. Kellogg, at the residence of her father, B. S. Kellogg, in Avon, the ceremony being performed by Rev. J. H. Twichell, of the Asylum Hill Congregational church, in Hartford, a very particular friend of the bridegroom. The bride wore a dress of white crape, imported expressly for this occasion from China, and elaborately trimmed with floss silk embroidery. Her brother and sister attended as groomsman and bridesmaid. After the ceremony a collation was served, in which Chinese delicacies were mingled with more substantial dishes of American style. Messrs. Yoh Shu Tung, manager, and Yung Yun Foo, teacher of the commission at Hartford, were present in national costume, but the groom, who long since adopted our style, appeared in full evening-dress. The bridal presents were numerous and costly. Mr. and Mrs. Wing left on the evening train for this city on a short wedding-trip.

Daniel Haurey, an Adams Express driver,

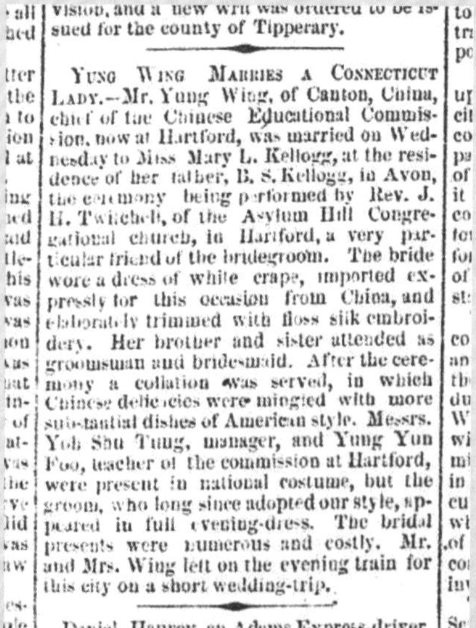

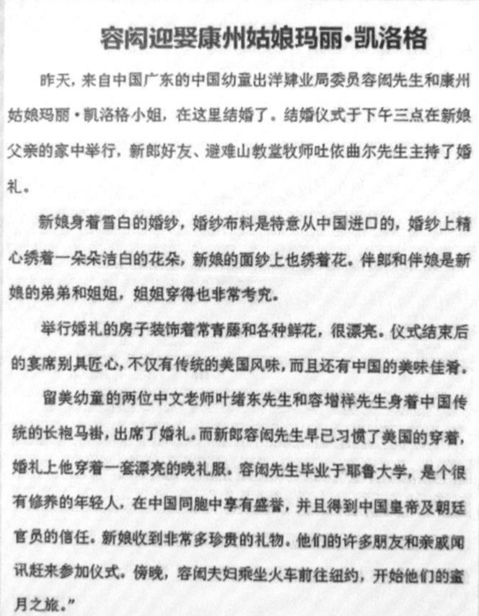

容闳迎娶康州姑娘玛丽·凯洛格

昨天，来自中国广东的中国幼童出洋肄业局委员容闳先生和康州姑娘玛丽·凯洛格小姐，在这里结婚了。结婚仪式于下午三点在新娘父亲的家中举行，新郎好友、避难山教堂牧师吐依曲尔先生主持了婚礼。

新娘身着雪白的婚纱，婚纱布料是特意从中国进口的，婚纱上精心绣着一朵朵洁白的花朵，新娘的面纱上也绣着花。伴郎和伴娘是新娘的弟弟和姐姐，姐姐穿得也非常考究。

举行婚礼的房子装饰着常青藤和各种鲜花，很漂亮。仪式结束后的宴席别具匠心，不仅有传统的美国风味，而且还有中国的美味佳肴。

留美幼童的两位中文老师叶绪东先生和容增祥先生身着中国传统的长袍马褂，出席了婚礼。而新郎容闳先生早已习惯了美国的穿着，婚礼上他穿着一套漂亮的晚礼服。容闳先生毕业于耶鲁大学，是个很有修养的年轻人，在中国同胞中享有盛誉，并且得到中国皇帝及朝廷官员的信任。新娘收到非常多珍贵的礼物。他们的许多朋友和亲戚闻讯赶来参加仪式。傍晚，容闳夫妇乘坐火车前往纽约，开始他们的蜜月之旅。”

○图4-19 图为3月8日《每日电讯报》关于容闳结婚的报道及其翻译稿

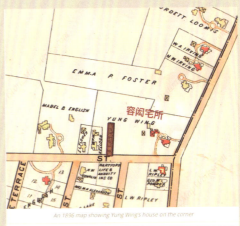

An 1896 map showing Yung Wing's house on the corner

○ 图4-20　容闳与玛丽的维多利亚式宅所位于哈特福德弗恩街与展望大道交界一角，玛丽哥哥威廉·凯洛克一家与他们比邻而居

○ 图4-21　容闳好友吐依曲尔牧师日记关于容闳婚礼的记载和他收集的当时报道

○ 图4-22　第四批留美幼童出国前在上海轮船招商总局门前合影

蔡绍基　　蔡廷干　　邓士聪　　梁如浩　　容尚谦　　容星桥　　谭耀勋

唐国安　　唐荣俊　　唐绍仪　　唐元湛　　唐致尧　　吴其藻　　张康仁

○ 图4-23　120名留美幼童中24名珠海籍幼童（其中10名幼童照片待发现：邓桂廷、黄有章、梁金荣、容尚勤、徐振鹏、唐荣浩、谭耀芳、盛文扬、张有恭、卓仁志）

○ 图4-24　图为徐润送三位堂弟与留美幼童一起自费赴美留学

（48）1876年/容闳48岁

被耶鲁大学授予"荣誉法学博士"，成为第一个被海外著名学府授予"荣誉法学博士"的中国人。"我个人视为是一项对中国的鼓励，视为是一种国家荣誉，是由世界上最年轻而进步的国家，颁赠给最古老而保守的人民，它鼓励中国去面向世界，并学习西方的文化、科学及宗教。"（摘自容闳给耶鲁大学校董庄士特回函）

8月，第七届世界博览会在美国费城举行。容闳组织留美幼童前往参观，幼童绘画、中英文双语文章《游美记》《哈佛书馆记》《庆贺百年大会序》《美国地图论》《风俗记》等作品参展。时任美国总统格兰特现场接见幼童。与会清廷代表团代表李圭，惊叹所见幼童"于千万人中言动自如，无畏怯态"，在其所著的《环游地球新录》中盛赞他们"西学所造，正未可量"。

6月10日，长子容觐彤出生，取名"Morrison Brown Yung"，纪念马礼逊学校和恩师布朗先生。

1876/at the age of 48

Yung wing was awarded an Honorary Doctorate of Law by Yale, becoming the first Chinese person to be awarded such an honor by a distinguished foreign university. Yung Wing organized the CEM students to attend the Centennial Exposition in Philadelphia. The students were personally received by President Ulysses S. Grant. On June 10, his eldest son was born and named Morrison Brown Yung in honor of the Morrison School and his mentor Mr. Brown.

o 图4-25 美国费城博览会展出的机械设备和大清国展区

o 图4-26　上图为1876年8月31日《纽约每日画报》关于留美幼童参观世界博览会的图片报道。下图为参加博览会的清廷代表团成员李圭及他所著的《环游地球新录》

YUNG WING.

CHINESE PUPIL RECITING.

o 图4-27 《斯克里布纳月刊》1876年11月登载的容闳素描和幼童画像

o 图4-28 幼年容觐彤和母亲的合影

（49）1877年/容闳49岁

3月，亲自选址并全程监制的幼童出洋肄业局三层大楼在哈特福德镇克林大道竣工，大楼由春田著名设计师戈登设计，清廷拨款五万美元。这是近代中国在国外的第一所官方建筑。"予之请于中国政府，出资造此坚固之屋以为办公地点，非为徒壮观瞻，盖欲使留学事务所在美国根深蒂固，以冀将来中政府不易变计以取消此事。"（摘自《西学东渐记》）

注意搜集欧美国家兵器研制信息，是年，倡议肄业局同仁捐款为国家购买新式枪炮。带头捐款13133美元，购买加特林机关枪，沙布兵枪及子弹等运送回国。李鸿章大为欣慰："该员等深明大义，捐助军需，自应量予奖叙。"

幼童定期到出洋肄业局学习四书五经，西化的举止言行与这里的中国老师产生冲突，容闳多次为学生辩护，被认为偏袒学生。"（学生）既离去故国而来此，终日饱吸自由空气，其平昔性灵上所受极重之压力，一旦排空飞去，言论思想，悉与旧教育不相符，好为种种健身之运动，跳踯驰骋，不复安行矩步，此皆必然之势，何足深怪。"（摘自《西学东渐记》）

1877/at the age of 49

In March, a three-story building for CEM headquarters was completed. This was the first official Chinese building constructed overseas in the modern era.

In the same year, Yung Wing donated $13,133 to purchase Gatling guns, Sharp's rifles, bullets, and other items to be transported back to China.

The young students regularly studied Chinese classics at the CEM building. They often clashed with their Chinese teachers due to their Westernized behavior and actions. Yung Wing defended the students and was accused of being biased towards them.

○ 图4-29 是年3月投入使用的幼童出洋肄业局大楼

○ 图4-30 左图为美国《哈泼斯周刊》关于容闳和幼童出洋肄业局大楼的报道。右图为《弗兰克·莱斯利周日杂志》刊载的幼童出洋肄业局大楼内部场景的插图

（50）1878年/容闳50岁

5月29日，向耶鲁大学捐赠个人收藏40种1237卷中国经典图书，这些书分四箱托运到耶鲁大学。包括《纲鉴易知录》、《三字经》、"四书"、"五经"、《山海经》、《康熙字典》、《李太白诗集》、《永乐大典》、《四库全书》、《古今图书集成》等等；其中《古今图书集成》一卷共计5024册，是现存保留完整的为数不多的版本之一。次年，又捐赠《大清律例全编》等442卷。耶鲁大学以这些书籍为基础，建立了美国第一个汉语文化中心——东亚图书馆。同年，推荐好友、卸任美国驻华公使卫三畏主持耶鲁大学"中国文化讲座"。卫三畏成为美国大学第一位汉学教授。

9月28日，在美国白宫蓝厅，与驻美公使陈兰彬向美国总统海斯递交国书。此时排华风渐起，国书称中美两国建交以来和睦相处，勿产生歧视，希望两国友谊长存。

挚友吐依曲尔牧师在耶鲁大学法学院演讲，介绍中国留美幼童计划。"容闳从头到脚，身上每一根神经都是爱国的，他热爱中国，信赖中国，确信中国会有灿烂的前程，配得上它的壮丽山河和伟大的历史。"（摘自吐依曲尔牧师在耶鲁大学法学院的演讲）

是年，詹天佑等五名留美幼童进入大学学习。

1878/at the age of 50

In May, Yung Wing donated 1,237 Chinese classic books to Yale. These books became the core of Yale's world-renowned East Asian Library, the first in the U.S. to focus on Asia.

On September 28, Yung Wing presented his credentials to President Rutherford Hayes. As anti-Chinese sentiment grew, he called for the preservation of friendship and the avoidance of discrimination.

In that year, five CEM students entered university in the US.

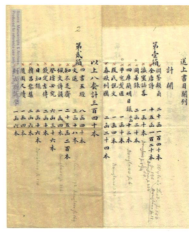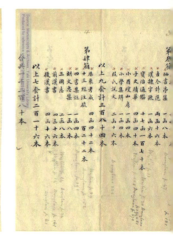

o 图4-31 容闳捐给耶鲁大学图书馆的中国典籍亲笔手写书目

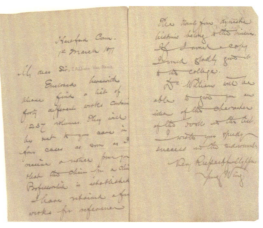

o 图4-32 3月1日，容闳致函耶鲁大学图书馆馆长范南，告知铁路托运1237卷中国经典，分四箱赠送给耶鲁大学。图为时任图书馆馆长范南和容闳给范南的信函

o 图4-33 上图为《弗兰克·莱斯利画报》登载的容闳（中立手持英文国书短须者）等人在白宫向美国总统海斯递交国书场景。下图为光绪皇帝致美国总统国书

○ 图4-34 图为在容闳推荐下主持
耶鲁大学"中国文化讲座"的卫三
畏博士

○ 图4-35 容闳（右）与好友吐依曲
尔牧师（左）

（51）1879年/容闳51岁

　　排华风潮越来越盛。容闳多次照会美国国务卿埃瓦茨，抗议美国同孚洋行替秘鲁掠运华工行为，谴责美国的排华运动。

　　山西发生灾荒，在哈特福德成立中国灭荒救济金劝募赈款，并再次要求美国政府退还《天津条约》额外赔款，赈灾山西。

　　留美幼童学业精进，《纽约时报》这样评价："这些从中国优秀家庭挑选出来的孩子表现出极高的天赋，处处受到人们的喜爱。"

　　是年，14名留美幼童考入美国大学读书，其中蔡绍基、谭耀勋和张康仁三人来自今珠海。

　　1月23日，次子容觐槐出生，取名"巴脱拉脱·容"，纪念美国挚友巴脱拉脱

1879/at the age of 51

As anti-Chinese sentiment grew stronger, Yung Wing lodged multiple protests to U.S. Secretary of State William Evarts, denouncing the anti-Chinese racism in the United States.

That year, fourteen students of CEM were admitted to American universities.

On January 23, Yung Wing's second son was born, named Bartlett Golden Yung in honor of his American friend Shubael Bartlett.

o 图4-36 初到美国的幼童照片

○ 图4-37　留美幼童组成的东方人棒球队在留美幼童肄业局前院合影。前排左起：陈钜镛、李桂攀、梁敦彦、邝詠钟；后排左起：蔡绍基、钟俊成、吴仲贤、詹天佑、黄开甲

○ 图4-38　留美幼童梁诚（前排右一）和棒球队队员合影

○ 图4-39　左图为耶鲁大学赛艇队舵手钟文耀（第二排居中者），右图为詹天佑（中排右一）和
棒球队队友合影

（52）1880年/容闳52岁

任驻美国、西班牙、秘鲁副公使，代行驻美公使职权，主要工作重心转到使馆。其间，多次照会美国国务卿，抗议中国轮船招商局"和众号"轮船在旧金山被超额征收船钞货税事件，在美国排华逆流中竭力维护华人利益和民族权益。是年，推荐中国第一个华侨百万富翁——陈芳为檀香山中国商董，后成为清朝政府驻夏威夷王国的第一任领事。

受郑观应委托在美国采购机器，招募技师，协助创办了中国第一家棉纺工厂——上海机器织布局。

是年，恩师布朗病逝于马萨诸塞州孟松，前往参加葬礼。

是年，出洋肄业局最后一任总办吴嘉善上任，认为留美幼童西化严重，数典忘祖，向总理衙门反映容闳放任学生，并向时任驻美公使陈兰彬建议，裁撤出洋肄业局和撤回留美幼童。

是年，21名留美幼童考入美国大学读书，其中唐国安、邓士聪两人来自今珠海。

1880/at the age of 52

Wu Jiashan, the last CEM Commissioner, harshly disciplined the young students and secretly reported Yung Wing to the Qing leaders. China's Minister, Chen Lanbin, proposed closing CEM and sending the students back to China.

That year, 21 CEM students were admitted to American universities.

○ 图4-40 图为容闳作为副公使工作的中国驻华盛顿使署，这是中国在美国的第一个外交机构

o 图4-41 图为位于今珠海凤山街道梅溪社区的陈芳家宅

o 图4-42 出任驻檀香山商董的陈芳

o 图4-43 容闳恩师布朗牧师遗照

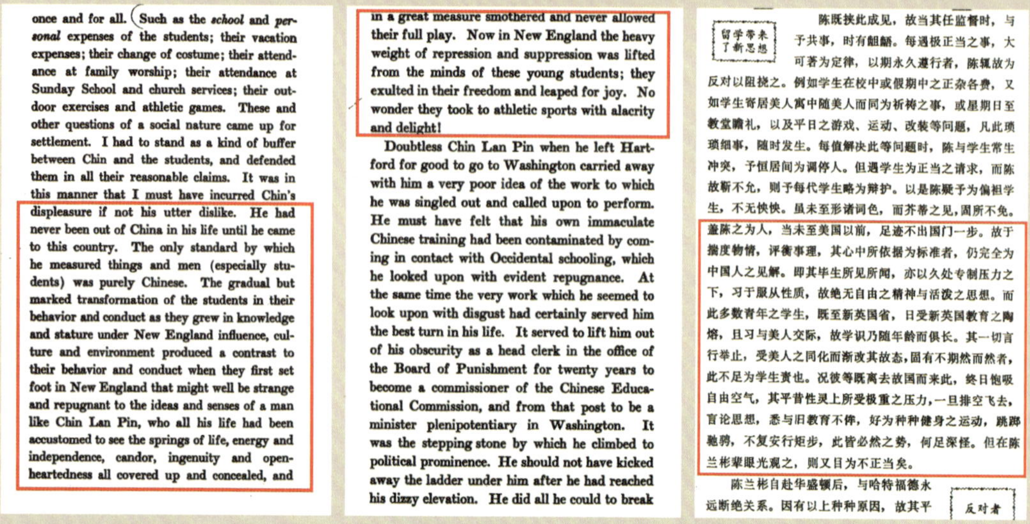

once and for all. Such as the *school* and *personal* expenses of the students; their vacation expenses; their change of costume; their attendance at family worship; their attendance at Sunday School and church services; their outdoor exercises and athletic games. These and other questions of a social nature came up for settlement. I had to stand as a kind of buffer between Chin and the students, and defended them in all their reasonable claims. It was in this manner that I must have incurred Chin's displeasure if not his utter dislike. He had never been out of China in his life until he came to this country. The only standard by which he measured things and men (especially students) was purely Chinese. The gradual but marked transformation of the students in their behavior and conduct as they grew in knowledge and stature under New England influence, culture and environment produced a contrast to their behavior and conduct when they first set foot in New England that might well be strange and repugnant to the ideas and senses of a man like Chin Lan Pin, who all his life had been accustomed to see the springs of life, energy and independence, candor, ingenuity and openheartedness all covered up and concealed, and in a great measure smothered and never allowed their full play. Now in New England the heavy weight of repression and suppression was lifted from the minds of these young students; they exulted in their freedom and leaped for joy. No wonder they took to athletic sports with alacrity and delight!

Doubtless Chin Lan Pin when he left Hartford for good to go to Washington carried away with him a very poor idea of the work to which he was singled out and called upon to perform. He must have felt that his own immaculate Chinese training had been contaminated by coming in contact with Occidental schooling, which he looked upon with evident repugnance. At the same time the very work which he seemed to look upon with disgust had certainly served him the best turn in his life. It served to lift him out of his obscurity as a head clerk in the office of the Board of Punishment for twenty years to become a commissioner of the Chinese Educational Commission, and from that post to be a minister plenipotentiary in Washington. It was the stepping stone by which he climbed to political prominence. He should not have kicked away the ladder under him after he had reached his dizzy elevation. He did all he could to break

留学带来了新思想

陈既挟此成见，故当其任监督时，与予共事，时有龃龉。每遇极正当之事，大可著为定律，以期永久遵行者，陈辄故为反对以阻挠之。例如学生在校中或假期中之正杂各费，又如学生寄居美人寓中随美人而同为祈祷之事，或星期日至教堂瞻礼，以及平日之游戏、运动、改装等问题，凡此琐琐细事，随时发生。每值解决此等问题时，陈与学生常生冲突，予恒居间为调停人。但遇学生为正当之请求，而陈故靳不允，则予每代学生略为辩护。以是陈疑予为偏袒学生，不无怏怏。虽未至形诸词色，而芥蒂之见，固所不免。盖陈之为人，当未至美国以前，足迹不出国门一步。故于揣度物情，评衡事理，其心中所依据为标准者，仍完全为中国人之见解。即其毕生所见所闻，亦以久处专制压力之下，习于服从性质，故绝无自由之精神与活泼之思想。而此多数青年之学生，既至新英国省，日受新英国教育之陶熔，且习与美人交际，故学识乃随年龄而俱长。其一切言行举止，受美人之同化而渐改其故态，固有不期然而然者，此不足为学生责也。况彼等既离去故国而来此，终日饱吸自由空气，其平昔性灵上所受极重之压力，一旦排空飞去，言论思想，悉与旧教育不侔，好为种种健身之运动，跳踯驰骋，不复安行矩步，此皆必然之势，何足深怪。但在陈兰彬辈眼光观之，则又目为不正当矣。

反对者

陈兰彬自赴华盛顿后，与哈特福德永远断绝关系。因有以上种种原因，故其平

○图4-44 容闳回忆录中，关于与陈兰彬、吴嘉善等观念冲突的记载

各區除銷本國外並可自派輪船運售於元山釜山
仁川及南洋各島則紗布之大利何難與泰西日本
諸國抗衡耶
余嘗與同志戴子撝太史龔仲人李韻亭兩觀察
蔡嵋青部郎經蓮珊主政集股銀四十萬公稟
傅相奏設上海織布局限期十年不准他人攙奪
如限期內有欲添設者或另開紡紗廠均由該局
代稟酌抽牌費津貼剏辦局用械請駐美公使容
純甫觀察於美國織布廠選一熟悉紡織誠實可
靠之洋匠來滬會商據云土花絲短恐於現成之

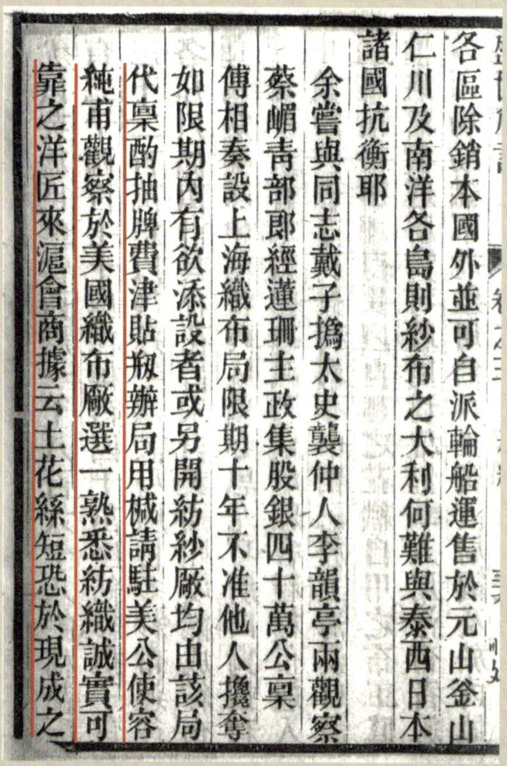

○图4-45　时任上海机器织布局总办的郑观应委托容闳在美国采购机器、招募技师的记载

（53）1881年/容闳53岁

　　陈兰彬、吴嘉善和国内守旧势力主张裁撤出洋肄业局。5月12日，总理各国事务衙门大臣奕䜣等奏请将出洋学生一律调回，奏折称："此等学生，若更令久居美国，必致全失其爱国之心，他日纵能学成回国，非特无益于国家，亦且有害于社会。"

　　受排华潮影响，容闳申请留美幼童入读西点军校和安纳波利斯海军学院的请求被美国国务院拒绝，加剧清廷不满。"予之所请既被拒绝，遂以此事函告总督。待接读总督覆书，予即知留学事务所前途之无望矣。"（摘自《西学东渐记》）

　　联系美国西方联合电报公司经理吉比·哈布尔，为周万鹏等25名留美幼童开设短期电报辅导班。这些学生后来成长为近代中国电报业的开拓者。

　　6月18日，清廷批准奕䜣等奏请的《将出洋学生一律调回折》。

　　请求耶鲁大学波特校长联络美国百余名大学校长和教育界知名人士，联名致函总理衙门："今学生如树木之久受灌溉培养，发荣滋长，行且开花结果矣，顾欲摧残于一旦而尽弃前功耶。"（摘自《美国各大学校长致总理衙门书》）。与美国文豪马克·吐温一起求助美国前总统格兰特，格兰特私信劝阻李鸿章。所有努力均告失败。

　　8月8日、8月23日和9月27日，94名留美幼童分三批先后归国。是时，已有43名留美幼童进入美国大学学习，另有17名等待大学录取通知书，仅詹天佑、欧阳庚两名幼童完成学业。

是年，容闳好友，出洋肄业局翻译邝其照在纽约出版《英文短语词典》，这是当时最完整的英文短语词典，也是中国人在美国出版发行的第一部书，得到哈佛、耶鲁、康奈尔等多所美国大学的肯定，被翻译成多国文字。

1881/at the age of 53

On June 18, the Qing court approved a memorandum calling for the recall of all students studying abroad. 94 CEM students were forced to return to China, even though 43 young students had already entered American universities.

Kuang Qizhao, Yung Wing's friend and translator for CEM, published *A Dictionary of English Phrases* in New York. This was the first book published by Chinese in the U.S. and was praised by the presidents of Yale, Harvard, Cornell, Johns Hopkins, and by other leading intellectuals.

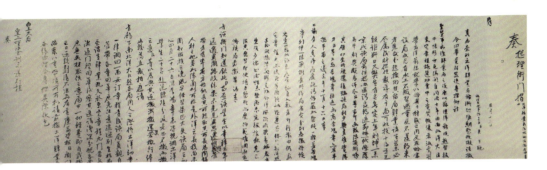

○ 图4-46 总理各国事务衙门大臣奕䜣等奏请的《将出洋学生一律调回折》

○ 图4-47 左图为11名入读耶鲁大学的留美幼童在离开美国加利福尼亚州前夕的合影。前排左起：梁敦彦、欧阳庚、钟文耀、陆永泉、刘家照；二排左起：陈钜镛、张康仁、陈佩瑚、祁祖彝、黄开甲；后排：詹天佑。右图为留美幼童在离开美国前举行的告别会上的签名

○ 图4-48詹天佑（四排
左二）和欧阳庚（二排左
一）的毕业合影

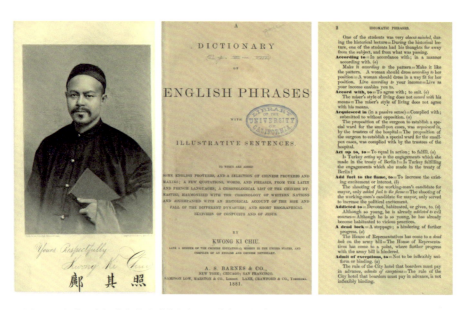

○ 图4-49 邝其照在纽约出版的《英文短语词典》，直到20世纪初依然是同类词典中最完整的

第五章　赤子拳拳

(1882—1899)

Unwavering Determination

（54）1882年/容闳54岁

代表清政府在哈特福德《每日新闻报》上刊登广告，出售幼童出洋肄业局大楼，处理后续事宜。3月，启程回国，向李鸿章述职销差。北京期间，向朝廷上奏禁止鸦片输入条陈。

留美幼童计划夭折，引起中外巨大反响。 2月13日，《纽约时报》报道称："可以肯定的是，清政府对这项事业意义的认识，远没有容闳博士那么深远。"

时任驻日本使馆参赞的容闳好友黄遵宪写下了纪事长诗《罢美国留学生感赋》，痛惜："蹉跎一失足，再遭终无期。目送海舟返，万感心伤悲。"

郑观应写下《赠美国肄业诸生并呈容沅浦邝容阶两教习》和《赠驻美国副使容纯甫观察》，责问："诸生游学将成业，公使何因促返槎。翻羡东瀛佳子弟，日新月盛愧吾华。"痛惜撤回留美幼童"因噎废食，功败垂成，殊为可惜也！"

是年，美国签署《排华法案》。留美幼童集中居住过的马萨诸塞州和康涅狄格州投下反对票。

1882/at the age of 54

Placed advertisements in the Hartford *Daily News* to sell the CEM building. In March, Yung Wing returned to China and reported to Li Hongzhang. Li submitted a memorial to the imperial court, requesting a ban on opium importation.

The termination of CEM triggered a huge response both domestically and internationally.

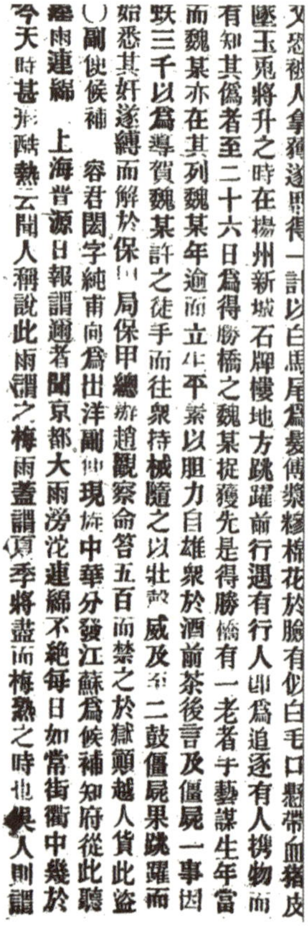
父恐被人拿獲遂思得一計以白馬尾爲髮傅漿糊棉花於臉有似白毛口鬚帶血豬皮
壓玉兎將升之時在揚州新城石牌樓地方跳躍前行遇有行人即爲追逐有人携物而
有知其僞者至二十六日爲得勝橋之魏某捉獲先是得勝橋有一老者于藝謀生年當
而魏某亦在其列魏某年逾而立生平素以胆力自雄衆於酒前茶後言及僵屍一事因
默三千以爲導賀魏某許之徒手而往衆持械隨之以壯聲威及至二鼓僵屍果跳躍而
始悉其奸遂縛而解於保甲局保甲總辦趙觀察命笞五百而禁之於獄顛越人貨此盜
（）副使候補　容君閎字純甫向爲出洋副使現旋中華分發江蘇爲候補知府從此聽
霪雨連綿　上海晋源日報謂邇者聞京都大雨滂沱連綿不絕每日如常街衢中幾於
今天時甚形酷熱云聞人稱說此雨謂之梅雨蓋謂[illegible]季將盡而梅熟之時也[illegible]人則謂

○ 图5-1　香港《循环日报》关于容闳回国的报道

○ 图5-2 1882年7月容闳上奏的《谢恩折》

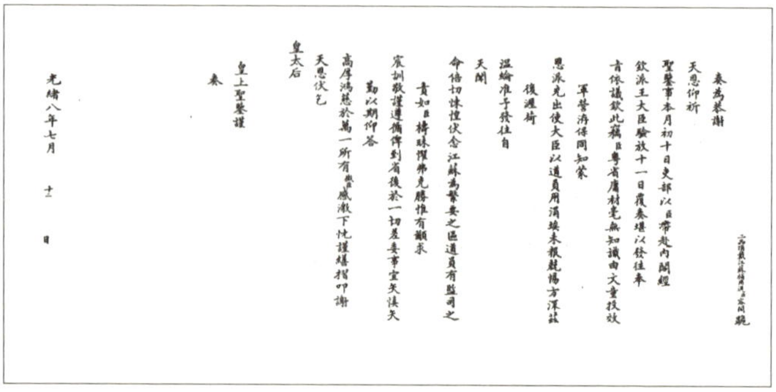
二品頂戴江蘇候補道臣容閎跪
奏爲恭謝
天恩仰祈
聖鑒事本月初十日吏部以臣帶赴內閣經
欽派王大臣驗放十一日覆奏堪以發往本
省依議欽此竊臣粵省庸材毫無知識由文童投效
軍營洊保同知銜
恩派充出使大臣以道員用涓埃未報兢惕方深茲
復邀
溫綸准予發往自
天闕
命倍切悚惶伏念江蘇爲繁要之區道員有監司之
責如臣檮昧譾弗克勝惟有籲求
宸訓敬謹遵循俾到省後於一切差委事宜矢慎矢
勤以期仰答
高厚鴻慈於萬一所有微臣感激下忱謹繕摺叩謝
天恩伏乞
皇太后
皇上聖鑒謹
奏
光緒八年七月　十二　日

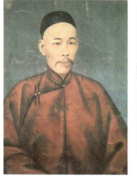

○ 图5-3 容闳好友、首任驻日参赞黄遵宪和他的《罢美国留学生感赋》

（55）1883年/容闳55岁

妻子病重，回到美国照顾妻子；夏天，偕妻前往弗吉尼亚州的诺福克避暑、疗养；冬天，偕妻到佐治亚州的亚特兰大休养、治病。"予妻体素柔弱，又因予常漫游，担心予遭遇不测，郁郁寡欢。余归国时，适有美教士某君告予妻曰：'容君此行，殊为冒险。恐中国政府或以留学事务所事，置之于法。'女子善怀，闻此不殊青天之霹雳，所以病也。"（摘自《西学东渐记》）

是年秋天，容闳亲自在老家南屏招收的留美幼童谭耀勋，从耶鲁大学毕业却不幸因肺病去世。他是当时敢于抗旨不归、留在美国的两个幼童之一。

是年12月，与容闳一起留学美国的黄胜，成为香港第一位华人太平绅士。

1883/at the age of 55

Yung Wing's wife fell ill. Yung Wing returned to the United States to take care of her. They went to Norfolk, Virginia for the summer so that she could recover. In the winter, they went to Atlanta for rest and medical treatment.

o 图5-4 佐治亚州的亚特兰大和弗吉尼亚州的诺福克，容闳陪同妻子在此两地疗养

o 图5-5　珠海籍留美幼童谭耀勋在哈特福德的墓碑，他被安葬在寄宿家庭卡特琳夫人家族墓地

（56）1884年/容闳56岁

偕妻在佐治亚州的亚特兰大继续休养、治病，后转往阿狄朗达斯。

是年，中法马尾海战爆发，六名留美幼童参战，其中薛有福、杨兆楠、黄季良、邝詠钟等四人以身殉国。

1884/at the age of 56

Accompanied by Yung Wing, Yung Wing's wife continued to rest and recover in Atlanta, Georgia. They then moved to the Adirondacks. That year, the Sino-French War broke out and six CEM students participated in the Battle of Fuzhou. Among them, four students sacrificed their lives for their country.

o 图5-6 在马尾海战中殉国的幼童薛有福（左一）、杨兆楠（左二）、邝咏钟（左三）、黄季良（左四）

o 图5-7 留美幼童
黄季良遗书

（57）1885年/容闳57岁

陪同妻子在阿狄朗达斯休养；冬天妻子胃病复发，转往新泽西州的萨姆维尔疗养。

是年4月，李鸿章上奏清廷，鉴于归国的留美幼童"均始终勤奋，日进有功"，建议对唐荣浩（今珠海唐家湾人）、徐振鹏（今珠海北岭村人）、黄开甲、梁普照等55名归国幼童"酌保官阶，给予顶戴"。

是年，广东南海人张荫桓出任美国、西班牙、秘鲁公使，留美幼童欧阳庚担任翻译。

1885/at the age of 57

Yung Wing accompanied his wife to New Jersey for treatment. In April, 55 CEM students were given official ranks and honors as they had all been diligent and successful in their studies.

In the same year, Zhang Yinhuan was appointed as Minister to the United States, Spain and Peru. Former CEM student Ouyang King served as his translator.

○ 图5-8　1885年4月，李鸿章呈送《奏请从优给奖美国回华学生及天津招募学习水师、鱼雷、水电、电报、医学生折》上奏光绪皇帝，建议对留美幼童"破格从优给奖，以昭激励"。归国幼童逐渐被清廷接纳。图为李鸿章及其奏折

○ 图5-9　新泽西州的萨姆维尔，容闳陪同妻子冬天在此疗养

（58）1886年/容闳58岁

5月28日，爱妻凯洛克因肾炎离世，年仅35岁，葬于哈特福德西带山公墓。"中年哀乐，人所难堪，吾则尤甚。今老矣，以吾妻留有二子，幸鲦而非独。"（摘自《西学东渐记》）

9月，在哈特福德接待新任驻美公使张荫桓，提出创设国家银行的建议，引导张荫桓前往纽海文考察枪械厂。张荫桓出使美国期间多次拜会容闳，交往深厚。"莼浦久游就美国，凡中外交涉事尚留心考究，尤侈言富强之略。"（摘自张荫桓《三州日记》）

10月，参加美国传教协会第40届年会并发表演讲。

1886/at the age of 58

On May 28, his beloved wife passed away due to nephritis at the young age of 35 and was buried at the West Mountain Cemetery in Hartford. Yung Wing was despondent.

In September, Yung Wing proposed the establishment of a national bank to Zhang Yinhuan. He accompanied Zhang as he inspected a New Haven gun factory.

egraph offices were open nothing could be learned of the cause of the delay.

Death of Mrs. Yung Wing.

Mrs. Yung Wing, formerly Mary Kellogg, wife of the former Chinese educational commissioner to this country, died Saturday in Hartford, Conn., of consumption, at the age of 35. Her marriage, in 1875, to a Chinaman attracted a good deal of attention. Miss Kellogg became acquainted with Yung Wing at the time that the colony of sons of wealthy Chinamen had quartered in Hartford and were being educated in the homes of several of the best people there. The marriage ceremony was attended by all the Chinese officials in this country. The presents were numerous, including many curios from China. For a number of years Mr. and Mrs. Wing have devided their time between Hartford and Washington, where Mr. Wing was connected with the Chinese embassy. He was graduated at Yale prior to being appointed educational commissioner, and afterwards became a naturalized citizen. Four children were born to the couple, two of whom are living. Mr. Wing contemplated a tried to China, but the failing health of his wife prevented it.

Three Bouncing Boys.

○ 图5-10　1886年6月4日美国《梅肯电讯报》关于容闳夫人去世的报道。报道称，中国幼童留美期间，有几个孩子寄宿在凯洛克小姐家中，因此缘分凯洛克小姐和容闳相识相恋。1875年她嫁给中国人容闳的时候，引起了很大的轰动。报道中还说到他们有4个孩子，有两个不幸夭折

Letter to Charles Alexis Kellogg, Sr. from Yung Wing, after the death of his wife, dated Hartford, Conn. June 13, 1886

Hartford, Conn.
13th June 1886

My dear Brother,

Here is a dress for Minnie, with ribbons for little Mary. Mary wore this dress but once. She made it just before going down to Summit. So it is perfectly new.

My heart is too heavy to write much. I have no ambition for anything. I am trying to reconcile myself to God's will & providence but my grief and sorrow are very great & I mourn over my beloved one day & night.

My whole life plan is completely broken up, & I do not know what to do with myself. Poor boys! their loss is even greater. They re deprived of their mother, her care, love, & moulding influence. They will realize it as they grow in years.

With love to all

Your brother in grief
Yung Wing

○ 图5-11　容闳在妻子去世一个多月后写给妻弟的信，诉说他悲恸沉痛、万念俱灰的心情。图为打印版信函。（容闳嫡孙容永成提供）

（59）1887年/容闳59岁

寓居哈特福德，抚育两子。"自一八八零年至一八八六年，为余生最不幸时期。毕生志愿，既横遭摧残（指教育计划）。同命之人，复无端夭折。顿觉心灰，无复生趣。两儿失母时，一才七龄，一才九龄。"（摘自《西学东渐记》）

3月，被推选为康州公理会俱乐部第十届年会会长。

7月，前往纽黑文出席留美幼童李恩富婚礼。是年，李恩富毕业于耶鲁大学，其所著英文版《我的中国童年》出版面世，讲述自己从中国一个南方小镇赴美留学的故事，披露了当时民众对留学的态度："事实上，父母很不希望让儿子出去离开他们那么长时间，并且去到他们并不了解的而且他们听说又是野蛮人居住的地方。"

1887/at the age of 59

He raised his two sons in Hartford. He writes, "From 1880 to 1886 was the most unfortunate period of my life. My life's ambition was shattered, and I suffered the same fate as others who were unjustly cut down in their prime. My heart sank and I lost all interest in life. "(from *My Life in China and America*).

In July, he attended CEM student Li Enfu's wedding. That year, Lee Enfu graduated from Yale University and published his English book *When I Was A Boy In China*.

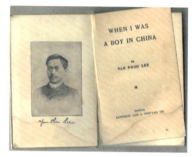

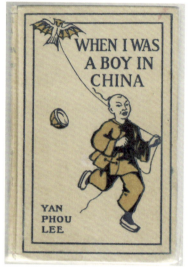

o 图5-12　3月17日《纽约时报》关于容闳被推选为康州公理会俱乐部第十届年会会长的报道

o 图5-13　留美幼童李恩富在纽约出版的英文自传原版《我的中国童年》

o 图5-14　图为李恩富之孙李理查在珠海参观容闳展览，并将祖父自传原版《我的中国童年》赠送给珠海博物馆

（60）1888年/容闳60岁

与驻美公使张荫桓来往频繁，11月接待张荫桓的再次来访。是年2月，珠海留美幼童唐国安在《中国时报》上发表了第一篇介绍幼童留美教育的文章——英文版《游美始末与收获》。文章首次披露了容闳促成留美幼童计划的艰辛过程，以及留美幼童计划夭折的内情。

5月18日，《纽约时报》报道毕业于哥伦比亚大学的珠海留美幼童张康仁获准美国执业律师资格，成为第一个美国华人律师。两年之后，因排华风潮，美国加州最高法院取消了张康仁的律师资格。2015年，在他被取消律师资格的125年以后，美国加州最高法院正式向张康仁追发加州律师执照，追认律师身份。

1888/at the age of 60

Yung Wing had frequent interactions with Zhang Yinhuan, the Chinese minister to the United States.

On May 18, the *New York Times* reported that Chang Hon Yen, a CEM student was granted a license to practice law in the United States, becoming the first Chinese American lawyer.

○图5-15 珠海南屏留美
幼童张康仁家庭照

○图5-16 图为
2015年加州法
院裁定书首页
及相关报道

○图5-17 图为天津第一份英
文报纸《中国时报刊》刊发的
留美幼童唐国安文章《游美始
末与收获》，文章详细介绍了
容闳促成留美幼童计划的过程
和幼童们在美国学习生活的情
况，以及最后计划夭折的内
情。文章还反映了幼童们回国
初期的磨难和他们在逆境中奋
起的努力

（61）1889年/容闳61岁

向驻美公使张荫桓推荐美国新式炸药，与美国军工厂谈判，为北洋水师购买火炮。

11月，前往克利夫兰参加留美幼童郑廷襄的婚礼。郑廷襄毕业于美国伍斯特理工学院，著名工程师，参与设计纽约布鲁克林大桥。由詹天佑主编的中国最早汉英工学字典《新编华英工学字汇》中的"郑氏车钩"便是以他的姓氏命名，专指他发明的连接火车车厢的车钩。

1889/at the age of 61

Recommended the purchase of new American armaments to Zhang Yinhuan. He negotiated with a U.S. military factory to purchase cannons for the Beiyang Navy. In November, he went to Cleveland to attend the wedding of CEM student Jang Ting Shan. Jang had graduated from Worcester Institute of Technology and participated in the design of the Brooklyn Bridge in New York.

bers, all earning good sums of money.

A Connecticut Girl Marries a Chinaman.

Jang Landsing, a native of China, residing in Cleveland, was married yesterday afternoon to Miss Nellie H. Sparks, daughter of Mrs. G. W. Sparks of Vernon, Conn. The ceremony was performed at the residence of the bride by the Rev. Joseph H. Twitchell of Hartford. The Hon. Yung Wing was among the guests. The groom came to this country in 1876 to the Chinese government school in Hartford. After the recall of the mission he remained in the service of the Chinese government as lieutenant in the navy. He returned to this country and was graduated from the Worcester polytecnic institute in 1887. Since then he has been employed by the Pratt & Whitney company of Hartford. He has recently accepted a place with the Brush electric light company of Cleveland.

○ 图5-18　左图为《美国华盛顿星报》关于留美幼童郑廷襄婚礼的报道（标红处），报道称，新郎是1876年作为第3批留美幼童来到哈特福德学习的中国人，他和康州姑娘结婚，容闳是参加婚礼的贵宾之一

○ 图5-19　留美幼童、美国伍斯特理工学院博士郑廷襄参与设计的纽约布鲁克林大桥

（62）1890年/容闳62岁

3月，给新任驻美公使崔国因发函，告知幼童出洋肄业局大楼出售情况。

圣诞节期间，部分留美幼童在国内第一次聚会，此后至1936年，这些幼童又聚会五次。

1890/at the age of 62

In March, Yung Wing sent a letter to the new minister in the United States about the sales of the CEM building. During Christmas, CEM students had their first reunion in China and would hold annual reunions until 1936.

○ 图5-20　1890年圣诞节部分留美幼童在天津聚会合影，这是留美幼童第一次聚会。后来，部分留美幼童又进行了多次聚会

○ 图5-21　1903年，上海聚会合影

○ 图5-22 1905年，在天津津海关道台衙门聚会合影

○ 图5-23　左图为1919年在母校"幼童出洋肄业沪局"原址聚会合影，17人的年龄相加正好1000岁，所以这次聚会合影被称为"千岁图"。右图为美国哈特福德报纸关于这次幼童聚会的相关报道

o 图5-24 1935年在上海聚会

o 图5-25 1936年，在上海最后一次聚会

（63）1891年/容闳63岁

在哈特福德抚育两个孩子。

是年，留美幼童欧阳庚与加州华裔骆丽莲结婚；10月，今珠海籍留美幼童唐绍仪代理驻朝鲜通商事宜，成为第一个走上政坛的留美幼童。

1891/at the age of 63

In October, Tang Shao Yi, a CEM student from Zhuhai, acted as an agent for trade in Korea.

○ 图5-26 容闳在哈特福德家中

○ 图5-27 唐绍仪和他的朝鲜妾室郑氏

（64）1892年/容闳64岁

多次抗议美国此起彼伏的排华风潮，倡议旅美华人组织抗议活动；10月，同乡好友唐廷枢在天津去世，享年60岁。13个国家驻津公使、商务代表参与护送灵柩回葬今珠海吉大。李鸿章在天津公祭仪式上说："中国可无李鸿章，但不可无唐廷枢。"

《北华捷报》称："唐廷枢的一生，标志着中国历史的一个时代，他的死是一个持久的损失。"

1892/at the age of 64

On multiple occasions, Yung Wing protested against frequent racism against Chinese in the US. He advocated for Chinese-Americans to organize protests against this racism. In October, his hometown friend Tang Tingshu passed away in Tianjin at the age of 60.

○ 图5-28 左图为唐廷枢与容闳学生时代合影，右为容闳。右图为位于今珠海唐家湾的唐廷枢故居观海楼遗址

○ 图5-29 唐廷枢遗像

○ 图5-30 1888年，北洋大臣李鸿章视察唐津铁路。作为李鸿章洋务运动的主将，开平矿务局总办唐廷枢亲自陪同。图为火车上合影。 前排左四为李鸿章，前排左二为唐廷枢

（65）1893年/容闳65岁

前往马萨诸塞州参加族弟、留美幼童容揆婚礼。

留美幼童钟文耀返回华盛顿任中国驻美国使署通译官。

留美幼童李桂攀与求学时期寄宿家庭房东的女儿伊丽莎白结婚，李桂攀在纽约出版的《英语不求人》一书，是最早在国外出版的中国人学英语的工具书之一。

1893/at age of 65

Yung Wing attended the wedding of CEM student Yung Kwai. CEM student Chung Mun Yew served as the secretary of the Chinese Embassy in the United States. CEM student Lee Kwai Pan married his American girlfriend. His book *Chinese-English Phrase Book in the Canton Dialect* was one of the earliest references books published abroad for the study of English.

o 图5-31　返回美国的留美幼童钟文耀曾是耶鲁大学赛艇队的舵手

o 图5-32　留美幼童李桂攀在纽约出版的《英语不求人》

五方不同文当今天下一家轮船铁路万里外若毗连而贸易交涉每苦於语言文字週不相通义未明而绪译多讹口欲宣则辞不达意留雕刻犹其後也然语言文字无不由浅而入深白可举一而反二神而明之存乎其人天下旁有扞格之事故會目之外交其或有涉獵嘉文而所識之書半非日用稱名之字則見過輒忘非急則治標之意也命肆業英文有年交近咲英语之圆於日用也緒以粤音聯口授印成小本什襲而藏卽西人習嘗言亦可開卷面得也子夏曰雖小道必有可觀者焉漫云乎哉

光緒十四年仲秋 步雲李桂攀識

光緒十四年仲秋刊

英語 不求人

紐約利泰棧售

o 图5-33　左图为容闳族弟、留美幼童容揆，他是当时敢于抗旨不归、留在美国的两名幼童之一。先后毕业于耶鲁大学、哥伦比亚大学。后成为驻华盛顿公使馆翻译。右图为容揆学生时期照片

（66）1894年/容闳66岁

7月25日，甲午战争爆发，通过驻美公使杨儒与湖广总督张之洞密切电报联系，提出多条抗击日本策略，老友蔡锡勇、留美幼童梁敦彦均为张之洞幕僚。张之洞采纳其中向英国借款购舰抄袭日本的策略；受张之洞委托，前往英国与伦敦银行财团商谈借款之事。借款事宜最后因清廷意见不一而落空。

"战事既开幕，予之爱国心油然而生，乃连发两书寄予友蔡锡勇君，蔡君前在公使馆为予之通译兼参赞者也。每书皆有条陈，规划战事，可使中国与日本继续战争，直至无穷期而力不竭。"（摘自《西学东渐记》）

是年，参加耶鲁同学毕业40周年纪念聚会。

是年，珠海留美幼童、容闳侄子容尚谦升任"环泰号"巡洋舰舰长，并率舰参加中日甲午战争。珠海留美幼童蔡廷干率领"福龙号"鱼雷艇参加黄海海战。沈寿昌、陈金揆、黄祖莲等三名留美幼童在甲午海战中为国捐躯。

1894/at the age of 66

On July 25, the first Sino-Japanese War broke out. Yung Wing communicated with Zhang Zhidong, the governor of Hubei and Hunan provinces. He proposed various strategies to resist Japan. At Zhang's request, Yung went to London to negotiate a loan with a consortium of banks.

He attended the 40th anniversary of his Yale class reunion.

Three CEM students sacrificed their lives for the country in the Battle of the Yellow Sea.

o 图5-34 容闳参加耶鲁同学毕业40周年聚会合影（前排右起第二人为容闳）

In 1894-5 war broke out between China and Japan on account of Korea. My sympathies were enlisted on the side of China, not because I am a Chinese, but because China had the right on her side, and Japan was simply trumping up a pretext to go to war with China, in order to show her military and naval prowess. Before the close of the war, it was impossible for me to be indifferent to the situation—I could not repress my love for China. I wrote to my former legation interpreter and secretary, two letters setting forth a plan by which China might prosecute the war for an indefinite time.

My first plan was to go over to London to negotiate a loan of $15,000,000, with which sum to purchase three or four ready built iron-clads, to raise a foreign force of 5,000 men to attack Japan in the rear from the Pacific coast—thus creating a diversion to draw the Japanese forces from Korea and give the Chinese government a breathing spell to recruit a fresh army and a new navy to cope with Japan. While this plan was being carried out, the government was to empower a commission to mortgage the Island of Formosa to some Western power for the sum of $400,000,000 for the purpose of organizing a national army and navy to carry on the war. These plans were embodied in two letters to Tsai Sik Yung, at that time secretary to Chang Tsze Tung, viceroy of Hunan and Hupeh. They were translated into Chinese for the Viceroy. That was in the winter of 1894. To my great surprise, Viceroy Chang approved of my first plan. I was authorized by cable to go over to London to negotiate the loan of $15,000,000.

中日战开两条献策

日本，非以祖国之故有所偏袒，其实曲在彼也。日人亦非不自知，特欲借此兴戎，以显其海陆军能力耳。战事既开幕，予之爱国心油然而生，乃连发两书寄予友蔡锡勇君，蔡君前在公使馆为予之通译兼参赞者也。每书皆有条陈，规划战事，可使中国与日本继续战争，直至无穷期而力不竭。

第一策：劝中国速向英伦商借一千五百万元，以购成铁甲三四艘，雇用外兵五千人，由太平洋抄袭日本之后，使之首尾不能相顾。则日本在朝鲜之兵力，必以分而弱。中国乃可乘此眼睛，急练新军，海陆并进，以敌日本。第二策与第一策同时并行：一面由中政府派员将台湾全岛，抵押于欧西无论何强国，借款四万万美金，以为全国海陆军继续战争之军费。时蔡为湖广总督张文襄（之洞）幕府，得书后以予策译为汉文，上之张督。此一八九四年冬间事也。

去伦敦活动借款

予初不意张督竟赞成予之第一策，立电来美，派予速赴伦敦借款一千五百万元。此时驻伦敦之中国公使，为李文忠属下之人。彼已先知予来英伦所任之事，故予亦无需另备特别公文，有事即可迳往谒公使。予抵伦敦不及一月，筹商借款已就绪，惟担保品尚未指定。予乃托公使转电政府，请以关税为抵押。不意总税务司赫德及直督李文忠不允所请，以为日本此时方要求一极大赔款，此关税指为日本赔款之抵押品，尤且虑其不足云。实则此亦随遁辞耳。盖李文忠素

o 图5-35 容闳回忆录中关于甲午战争抗敌策略的记载

o 图5-36 惨烈的甲午海战现场

o 图5-37 图为海战中殉国的留美幼童陈金揆（左）和沈寿昌（右）

Admiral Tsai Ting-kan
蔡廷幹字耀堂
(Ts'ai T'ing-kan)

○ 图5-38 珠海留美幼童蔡廷干和他率领参战的福龙号鱼雷艇（见下图）

○ 图5-39 蔡廷干晚年完成的《唐诗英韵》，1932年由美国芝加哥大学出版社出版，是由中国人编译向西方介绍我国古典诗歌的首部英文作品

（67）1895年/容闳67岁

做回中国准备。请妻兄凯洛克博士担任两个孩子监护人，安排幼子容觐槐寄宿吐依曲尔牧师家。

3月，接受两江总督张之洞邀请返回上海，留美幼童黄开甲、唐元湛、牛尚周等举行欢迎会。向张之洞提出"完全执行政策"，包括聘用外国人辅政、普及国民教育、开放女子教育等若干富强新政策，虽然当时未被采纳，但是后来大都体现在张之洞在湖北实施的洋务新政里面。而后以江南洋务委员身份闲置南京。三个月后辞掉职务。"在中国官场中，必谓此举为不敬上官，予则不暇计矣。此三月内，每月领薪百五十元，而无一事可为，无异于一挂名差使。"（摘自《西学东渐记》）

1895/at the age of 67

In March, Yung Wing returned to Shanghai at the invitation of Zhang Zhidong and proposed several new policies for strengthening the country. Later, he remained idle in Nanjing as a member of the Jiangnan Arsenal Board. After three months, he resigned from the position.

o 图5-40 左图为出生于贵州贵阳的晚清重臣张之洞。右图为《北华捷报》8月16日关于容闳拜访两江总督张之洞并留在南京的报道，报道中还介绍了容闳的生平

o 图5-41 与幼童上海合影（左起：吴其藻、杨昌龄、容闳、吴仰曾）

o 图5-42 左图为容闳与吐依曲尔牧师在哈特福德。右图为吐依曲尔牧师日记本中关于容闳应张之洞邀请回国效力的报刊文章剪贴

（68）1896年/容闳68岁

寓居同乡好友徐润（今珠海北岭村人）在上海创办的同文书局，这是中国人自办的第一家近代石版印刷机构。

翻译美国《国家银行法》及其相关法律，留美幼童黄开甲参与其中。北京拜会时任总理衙门大臣、户部左侍郎张荫桓，游说开办国家银行，得到户部尚书翁同龢认可。

撰写国家银行计划及相关章程，经户部征求意见后，形成《仿泰西设立银行条陈》上报朝廷。这是近代中国第一个以西方银行法和有关条规为蓝本、最完备最详尽的兴办银行方案，但是银行计划遭他人作梗而失败。

结识维新派人物梁启超和康有为。是年秋，维新派机关报《时务报》先后刊发了《容观察请创办银行章程》《容观察续拟银行条陈》，披露容闳银行计划。"究国家银行计划失败之原因，亦不外乎中国行政机关之腐败而已。尊自太后，贱及吏胥，自上至下，无一不以贿赂造成。"（摘自《西学东渐记》）

制定铁路计划，向总理衙门呈递《津镇铁路条陈》《实务报》《湘报》等刊发，这一条陈是中国近代最早倡议引进外商投资、参与创办实业的方案。

春夏之交，容闳回到家乡南屏，为在美国的两个儿子补行入族仪式。长子取族名咏兰，幼子取族名嘉兰。

是年，珠海籍留美幼童蔡绍基参与创办近代中国第一所现代意义上的大学——北洋大学堂（今天津大学）。

是年，《耶鲁大学1854班刊》出版，该年级校友容闳记载在册。

1896/at the age of 68

Living in Shanghai, Yung Wing drafted and submitted a plan to the imperial court for the establishment of a national bank. This was the first and most complete plan for a Western-style bank in modern China. Yung Wing also submitted a proposal for a Tianjin-Pukou railway to the Grand Council. This was one of the earliest proposals in modern China to introduce foreign investment and cooperation in business. Both plans were published in a newspaper.

In the same year, CEM student Tsai Shou Kee participated in the establishment of the first modern university in China, the Beiyang College (now Tianjin University).

○ 图5-43 容闳同乡好友徐润和他的同文书局

○ 图5-44 图为翁同龢和他的日记中关于对容闳的记载："江苏候补道容闳号纯甫，久住美国，居然洋人矣。然谈银行颇得要领。"

○ 图5-45 《时务报》第九册刊发了《容观察闳请创办银行章程》，图为第九册目录。条陈包括《银行总纲四条》《总行章程十二条》《分行章程二十四条》和《续拟银行条成六条》

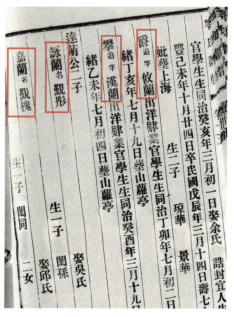

o 图5-46 珠海籍留美幼童蔡绍基（今珠海北岭村人）和他参与创建的北洋大学堂（今天津大学）

o 图5-47 《容氏谱牒》中关于容闳两个儿子和侄子的记载，其中"咏兰名觐彤"为容闳长子，"嘉兰名觐槐"为容闳次子

（69）1897年/容闳69岁

与清廷重臣张荫桓及清廷外交官、留美幼童梁诚一起代表清政府前往伦敦出席维多利亚女皇登基60周年钻石禧庆典。

举荐唐山开平矿务局矿冶工程师、留美幼童邝荣光主持湖南煤矿勘察工作。邝荣光成为湘潭煤矿的发现者并绘制了中国第一幅地质图《直隶省地质图》

是年，留美幼童唐荣俊（今珠海唐家湾人）在上海创办最早的华人自来水厂——上海内地自来水公司。

1897/at the age of 69

Yung Wing represented the Qing court at Queen Victoria's Diamond Jubilee celebration in London.

In the same year, CEM student Tang Wing Chun founded Shanghai's earliest Chinese-owned water company.

o 图5-48 维多利亚女皇登基60周年钻石禧庆典

o 图5-49 珠海籍留美幼童唐荣俊（左）和他创办的上海内地自来水公司内部图（右）

（70）1898年/容闳70岁

正月二十一日，总理衙门批准容闳的《兴筑津镇铁路条陈》，《申报》全文刊载。然而实施中再次遭遇失败。"予之种种政策，既皆无效，于是予之救助中国之心，遂亦至此而止矣。"（摘自《西学东渐记》）

是年，参加康有为在北京发起的保国会成立大会，参与康梁维新派重大活动的策划。康有为在给光绪皇帝的奏折中，推荐容闳担任外事联络职务。9月21日，维新变法失败，被清廷通缉而出逃，一同与容闳在夫子庙寓所共议变法大计的谭嗣同等六名维新志士惨遭杀害。"予之寓所，一时几变为维新党领袖之会议场。迨一八九八年秋，遂有政变之事。因此变局，光绪被废，多数维新党之领袖，皆被清廷捕杀。予以素表同情于维新党，寓所又有会议场之目，故亦犯隐匿党人之嫌，不得不迁徙以逃生。乃出北京，赴上海，托迹租界中。"（摘自《西学东渐记》）

1898/at the age of 70

Yung Wing participated in "The Hundred Days Reform" in Beijing. The house he lived in became the meeting place for the Reform Party leaders. When the reform movement failed, Yung Wing went into hiding after the Qing court issued a request for his arrest. He fled Beijing, and travelled to Shanghai, where he hid in the foreign concession.

o 图5-50《申报》载容闳
《兴筑津镇铁路条陈》

o 图5-51 与容闳交往至密的维新派
领袖康有为（左）和梁启超（右）

（71）1899/容闳71岁

　　逃出北京，托迹上海租界。年底，赴香港，蛰居香港皇后大道寓所。

　　是年，留美幼童刘玉麟出任驻新加坡领事，珠海留美幼童唐国安等人参加耶鲁同学在上海的聚会。

1899/at the age of 71

　　Fleeing Peking, Yung Wing sought refuge in the Shanghai concession. At the end of the year, he arrived in Hong Kong. CEM student Liu Yu lin was appointed as Consul in Singapore.

○ 图5-52 图为19世
纪初期容闳寓居的
香港皇后大道

○ 图5-53 左图为出任驻新加坡领事的留美幼童刘玉麟，他在唐绍仪任中山模范县县长时，担任
中山县第一区自治筹备所所长。右图为耶鲁同学会在上海的聚会，留美幼童唐元湛（左一）、唐
国安（左三）、曾恭笃（左四）、朱宝奎（右二）

第六章 共和之光

(1900—1912)

The Light of Republicanism

（72）1900年/容闳72岁

蛰居香港。经留美幼童、兴中会会员容星桥（今珠海南屏人）引荐，在香港与革命党人杨衢云、谢缵泰共谋复兴大业。

3月，赴新加坡，与康有为、新加坡富商邱菽园以及台湾爱国诗人丘逢甲共商起兵事宜。丘逢甲赠诗三首给容闳。

7月，与唐才常、严复等在上海成立中国国会，被推选为会长，用英文起草了《中国国会宣言》，提出使中国"立二十世纪最文明之政治模范"的理想。

张之洞发出《宣布康党逆迹并查拿自立会匪首片》，公开通缉容闳。9月1日赴日本避难，化名"秦西"，与化名"中山樵"的孙中山和化名"平田普"的容星桥同乘"神父丸"号轮船赴日，自此从维新走向革命。

是年，义和团运动在中国北方部分地区达到高潮，清朝向西方列强宣战。八国联军占领北京。

1900/at the age of 72

In July, Yung Wing was elected president and drafted the "Declaration of the Chinese National Assembly" in English，proposing to make China "the most civilized political model for the 20th century."

Qing court issued a notice and publicly declared Yung Wing a fugitive. On September 1, he fled to Japan with Sun Yat-sen and CEM student Yung Yew Huan, marking his transition from being part of the reform movement to joining the revolutionary cause.

○ 图6-1 八国联军侵占北京。图为他们在攻打东交民巷

○ 图6-2 左图为1900年的孙中山，在这一年，他和容闳相遇。右图为孙中山亲自介绍加入兴中会的容闳族弟、留美幼童容星桥

（73）1901年/容闳73岁

年初到台湾，处理多年前投资购买的基隆地产遗留问题。居台粤人纷纷前往拜访。1月15日《台湾日日新报》载："前清国出使美国大臣容闳，粤东知名士也，戊戌之间为南清改革派领袖，近以漫游台湾，下榻于台北义和洋行，盖买办容其年，其犹子也。容君识论风生，年已七十，复有矍铄是翁之概。粤人羁旅台北其未尝见之者，闻容君来，皆愿一识荆州以为快。"其间，面见台湾总督日本人儿玉源太郎。总督告知已收到通缉公文，要求把容闳逮捕送回中国。容闳从容回答赢得总督敬重，化险为夷。"予今在阁下完全治权之下，故无论何时，阁下可从心所欲，捕予送之中政府。予亦甚愿为中国而死，死固得其所也。"（摘自《西学东渐记》）

是年，珠海籍留美幼童、时任山东洋务局委员唐绍仪参与创办中国第二所国立大学——山东大学堂。

是年，《辛丑条约》签订，中国赔偿十一国4亿5千万两白银，史称"庚子赔款"。

1901/at the age of 73

Traveled to Taiwan and met with the Japanese governor-general Kodama Gentaro. The governor informed him that he had received a warrant for his arrest. Yung Wing provided a good, calm reply, earning the respect of the governor and averting disaster.

That year, CEM student Tang Shao Yi, participated in the establishment of Shandong University, China's second national university.

o 图6-3 近代中国第二所国立大学山东大学堂在济南成立，图为光绪皇帝对《山东大学堂章程》的朱批

o 图6-4 《辛丑条约》签署现场

（74）1902年/容闳74岁

年初，最后一次回到故乡南屏，拜祭父母，看望乡亲。居住在南屏容氏宗祠二楼阁楼。

5月，从香港启程赴美。美国认为容闳美国公民身份失效，拒绝容闳赴美定居。在留美幼童张康仁帮助下，从旧金山入境。

6月，参加幼子容觐槐耶鲁大学毕业典礼。

展望大道宅所已卖掉，租住哈特福德里迈特尔街12号。受排华潮影响，此后十年频频迁居，先后住过里迈特尔街16号、阿西鲁姆道771号、沙京街310号、阿特伍德街16号、沙京街284号等。

与革命党人谢缵泰等密切来往，收到谢缵泰从香港寄来的密码本。

是年，留美幼童曹嘉祥出任天津巡抚总局首任总办，创立中国近代警察制度。

1902/at the age of 74

Returned to his hometown of Nanping for the last time.

In June, he attended Yale University's graduation ceremony as an honorary guest of his younger son. That year, CEM student Taso Ka Hsiang was appointed as the first director of the Tianjin Police Bureau, establishing China's first modern police system.

○ 图6-5 出任天津巡抚总局首任总办的留美幼童曹嘉祥成为中国现代警察制度的创始人。上图为曹嘉祥留美期间持猎枪照。下图为清末明信片——天津太平庄的巡警

55. - TIEN-TSIN. - Policemans de Ta-Ping-Chouan

o 图6-6　《路易斯日报》1902年6月14日关于容闳返回美国的报道。报道称，过去几十年中，容闳博士在中国的事务中扮演了非常重要的角色。最近因为卷入戊戌变法被通缉。报道还说容闳对在中国刚刚经历的这段危险讳莫如深，不愿提及

o 图6-7　现藏于美国康涅狄格州立图书馆的容闳1902年日记，记录了容闳上半年在香港、澳门以及家乡等地的社会交往以及下半年返回美国的情况。左一为日记封面，左二为扉页备忘录，左三为回乡记载

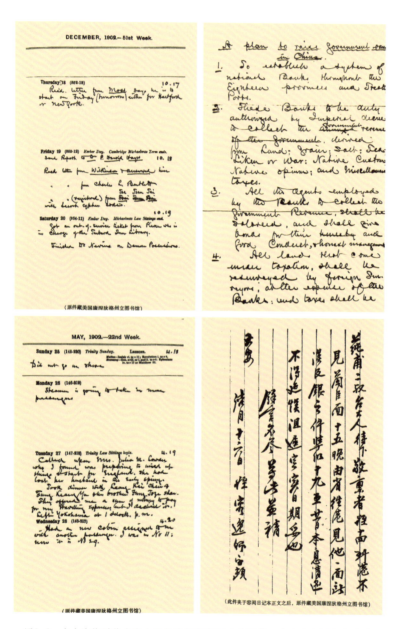

（原件藏美国康涅狄格州立图书馆）

（原件藏美国康涅狄格州立图书馆）

（此件夹于容闳日记本正文之后，原件藏美国康涅狄格州立图书馆）

○ 图6-8　左上为收到革命党人谢缵泰所寄密码本的记载。右上为中国发行政府公债计划方案。左下为在横滨与梁启超及冯镜如兄弟共进午餐的记载。右下为夹在日记本中侄儿容逸卿写给容闳的便条。在此期间，容逸卿为容闳打理日常事务

（75）1903/容闳75岁

4月，接待流亡美国的梁启超拜访，出席梁启超演讲会并引荐留在美国的昔日幼童。5月，陪同梁启超参观哈佛大学。"（容闳）先生今年七十六，而矍铄犹昔，舍忧国外无他思想，无他事业也。余造谒两时许，先生所以教督之劝勉之者良厚，策国家之将来，示倪论之方针，条理秩然，使人钦佩。"（摘自梁启超《新大陆游记节录》）

是年，留美幼童梁诚出任驻美公使。《纽约时报》以"新任中国驻美公使梁诚验证了容闳的留学教育计划对他祖国的贡献"为题报道梁诚履职。

1903/at the age of 75

In April, he attended a lecture by Liang Qichao.

Because of anti-Chinese racism, he frequently moved from place to place.

That year, CEM student Liang King Ao was appointed as the Chinese Ambassador to the United States. The *New York Times* writes that the appointment of a CEM student demonstrates that Yung Wing's study abroad program was highly effective.

○ 图6-9 梁诚在驻华公使馆办公室和美国媒体对他的报道。报道还刊发了他1881年在美国留学的
照片

○ 图6-10 容闳在美国的居所之一

（76）1904/容闳76岁

寓居哈特福德。参加在纽约举办的国际仲裁会议第十届年会闭幕式，并发表关于中国的演说。

康有为之女康同璧赴美留学，寄居容闳家中半年。

4月，美国圣路易斯博览会开幕，留美幼童黄开甲担任中国馆副监督主持开馆事宜。慈禧太后巨幅画像首次参展，留美幼童、驻美公使梁诚在展览结束后将画像赠送美国总统。

珠海留美幼童唐绍仪以"钦差议约全权大臣"身份赴印度与英国就西藏问题进行谈判，成功地捍卫了中国在西藏的主权。后来，随行参赞梁士诒之女与容闳长子容觐彤成婚，容梁两家结秦晋之好。

1904/at the age of 76

Living in Hartford, he attended the 10th annual meeting of the International Arbitration Conference in New York and gave a speech.

In April, the St. Louis World's Fair opened. CEM student Wong Kai Kah served as the deputy supervisor of the Chinese Pavilion. CEM student Tang Shao Yi went to India to negotiate with the British on the Xi Zang's issue and succeeded.

o 图6-11 留美幼童黄开甲在博览会现场（图片居中者）和留美时期的照片

o 图6-12 在博览会展出的慈禧太后画像

o 图6-13 唐绍仪在印度谈判时合影（中为唐绍仪，左一为容永成外祖父梁士诒）。本照片由容闳嫡孙容永成提供

（77）1905/容闳77岁

寓居哈特福德，与康有为父女联系频繁。

6月15日，陪同康有为、美国军事家荷马·李等前往白宫拜会美国总统西奥多·罗斯福。

驻美公使梁诚查实美国所得庚子赔款远远高于实际损失，开始动议追回多余赔款。"兹查此项赔款，除美国商民传教士应领各款外，实溢美金二千二百万元……宜声告美国政府，请将此项赔款归还，以为广设学堂、派遣游学之用。"（摘自《驻美公使梁诚致外务部函（1905年5月13日）》）

留美幼童温秉忠、珠海留美幼童唐元湛、珠海唐宝锷随同清廷五大臣出洋考察，这是清廷第一次官方出洋考察团。

留美幼童詹天佑出任京张铁路局会办兼总工程师。9月，主持修建中国自主设计建造的第一条铁路干线——京张铁路，被誉为中国铁路之父。

珠海留美幼童、时任山海关内外铁路总局总办梁如浩将因八国联军入侵中断的中国第一所铁路学堂复校迁址唐山，成立山海关内外路矿学堂（今西南交通大学前身），留美幼童周寿臣、留美幼童方伯樑担任首任会办、首任监督。

是年，清廷终结延续千年的科举制度，以留学生考试取而代之。珠海留美幼童、时任外务部右侍郎唐绍仪被任命为主考官，此举极大促进了中国近代化发展。

1905/at the age of 77

Living in Hartford, he accompanied Kang Youwei and American military strategist Homer Lea to meet with U.S. President Theodore Roosevelt.

CEM student Jeme Tien oversaw the construction of China's first railway line built with independent design and construction, earning him the title "Father of Chinese Railroads."

CEM student Liang Cheng argued that the indemnity paid to the US after the Boxer Rebellion far exceeded the actual losses suffered by China and proposed that the US return the excess amount.

○图6-14 驻美公使梁诚致外务部函，首次提出追回庚子多余赔款、用于广设学堂派遣游学用

○图6-15　左图为朝廷颁发废除科举考试的《立停科举以广学校谕》和弃置的南京科举考场。右图为担任科举考试废除之后首次留学生考试主考官的留美幼童唐绍仪

○ 图6-16 康有为女儿康同璧和容闳给她的亲笔信

○ 图6-17 詹天佑学生时期的照片、任京张铁路总办时的照片以及京张铁路通车典礼（前排右一站立者为詹天佑）

o 图6-18 詹天佑家庭照，其妻谭菊
珍为今珠海南屏人，为留美幼童谭
耀勋妹妹

o 图6-19 五大臣出洋考察团在美国，前排
右一为领队端方，二排右二为留美幼童驻
美公使梁诚，三排居中为随团翻译留美幼
童温秉忠

○ 图6-20　上图为创办于1896年的中国第一所铁路学堂——山海关北洋铁路官学堂。左下图为梁
如浩，右下图为其学生时期照片

（78）1906年/容闳78岁

寓居哈特福德。

是年，珠海留美幼童蔡绍基参与中国第一次大规模邀请外宾观摩的开放性军事大演习——彰德会操，负责"总理接待各国观操人员一切事物"，参加观摩的外宾有来自英、美、俄、法、德、意、奥、荷、日等国的武官和世界知名报纸的记者。

同年4月，美国旧金山发生大地震，时任旧金山总领事的留美幼童欧阳庚组织人员救灾。

1906/at the age of 78

Living in Hartford. Former CEM student Tsai Shou Kee participated in China's first modern military exercise and was responsible for diplomacy. In April , a major earthquake occurred in San Francisco, and CEM student Ouyang King, who was then the Consul General in San Francisco, organized relief efforts.

○ 图6-21　图为留学期间的蔡绍基（左）、观摩彰德会操的外国武官和《伦敦新闻画报》刊发的被检阅的新军

○ 图6-22　左图为哈特福德街景。右图为容闳晚年居所之一，美国哈特福德阿特伍德街16号

（79）1907年/容闳79岁

寓居哈特福德。9月，向革命党人谢缵泰提出了一系列促进中国革命成功的方案。

是年，清廷破格给詹天佑、吴仰曾、邝荣光等三名留美幼童"各科进士出身"。

留美幼童周寿臣成为香港太平绅士，后被委任为香港行政局首位华人参事，香港南部的寿臣山就是以他的名字命名的。

1907/at the age of 79

Living in Hartford, Yung wing proposed to revolutionary Xie Zuantai a series of plans to promote the success of the Chinese revolution. That year, the Qing court granted the title of "jinshi" (successful candidate in the highest imperial examinations) to three students of CEM.

Former student of CEM, Chow Chang Ling became a member of the Hong Kong Legislative Council and the first Chinese person to hold such a position.

○ 图6-23 1907年，容闳
在哈特福德家中

○ 图6-24 和容闳联系密切的
革命党人谢缵泰

○ 图6-25　周寿臣和他幼童期间照片

○ 图6-26　图为周寿臣担任香港参事的相关报道

○ 图6-27　图为香港以周寿臣名字命名的寿臣山一带地理位置图。他的住宅松涛居门前道路被命名为寿山村道，环山的道路命名为寿臣山道。

○ 图6-28　留美幼童邝荣光（前左一）、唐国安（前左二）、梁普照（前左三）、吴仰曾（前左四）在开滦煤矿合影。他们成为中国最早的矿冶工程师

（80）1908年/容闳80岁

寓居哈特福德。参与共和革命，说服美国军事家荷马·李和美国银行家布思等友人，支持孙中山先生。

在留美幼童梁诚等推动下，美国国会通过法案，授权西奥多·罗斯福总统退还中国"庚子赔款"中超过美方实际损失的部分，用于中国学生的赴美留学，史称"庚款奖学金计划"。时任外务部右侍郎、留美幼童梁敦彦代表清廷签署退款协议书，时任奉天巡抚、留美幼童唐绍仪以致谢专使大臣身份，赴美致谢，并向时任美国总统罗斯福赠送《钦定古今图书集成》一套。

1908/at the age of 80

Living in Hartford, Yung Wing convinced his American friends, including the military strategist Homer Lea and the banker Jacob Schiff, to support Dr. Sun Yat-sen.

The U.S. decided to return to China the portion of the Boxer Indemnity exceeding the actual American losses for Chinese students studying in America. The program was called the "Boxer Indemnity Scholarship Program". CEM student Liang Dunyan signed the agreement on behalf of the Qing court, while CEM student Tang Shao Yi travelled to the United States as a special envoy to express gratitude.

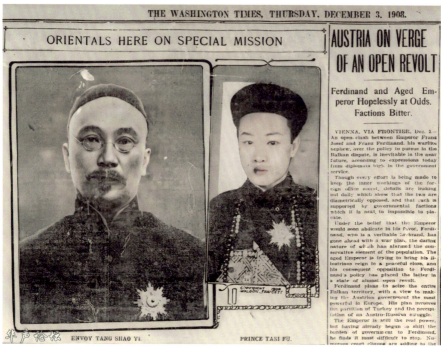

○ 图6-29 《华盛顿时报》关于唐绍仪率团赴美致谢的报道，左为唐绍仪，右为庆亲王次子载溥

○ 图6-30 唐绍仪携带到美国的致谢礼物是徐润1894年印刷完工的《钦定古今图书集成》，全套5044册，这是中国规模最大的百科全书，现藏于美国国会图书馆。右图为本书作者徐惠萍2016年在美国国会图书馆亲见这套书

（81）1909年/容闳81岁

寓居哈特福德，参加在哈特福德召开的中国留学生同盟联会并发表演讲。

11月，英文回忆录*My Life in China and America*由美国纽约亨利·霍尔特公司出版。1915年，这本书传到中国，被译为《西学东渐记》，成为研究近代中西文化交流和中国近代化之路的经典文本。"西学东渐"一词，便是由该书而来。

是年，清廷设立"游美学务处"，启动庚款奖学金计划，珠海籍留美幼童唐国安出任游美学务处坐办，珠海籍留美幼童唐元湛出任游美学务处驻沪委员，留美幼童容揆担任留学生游美监督处监督。

10月，唐国安带领第一批47名庚款学生赴美国留学。"庚款奖学金计划"持续到1949年，更大规模地延续了容闳的留学教育计划，数千名中国青年负笈求学，救亡图存，成为中国从封闭走向开放、从落后走向富强的中坚力量。

"正是由于他们，原先的留学事务所复活了，虽然形式上也有变更，因此如今人们可以看到中国学生，翩翩联袂从遥远的天涯海角来到欧美接受科学教育。"（摘自《西学东渐记》）

是年，长子容觐彤遵父命回中国报效。后被孙中山先生聘为内务部技师，主持撰写第一部《中国矿业条例草案》。

1909/at the age of 81

Yung Wing participated in the Chinese Students' Alliance Convention held in Hartford and delivered a speech. In November, his English memoir *My Life in China and America* was published in New York, and was translated into Chinese in 1915.

This year, the Qing started the "Boxer Indemnity Scholarship Program." In October, CEM student Tang Kwo On led the first group of 47 students to America. The Program continued and expanded Yung Wing's original educational plan, allowing thousands of Chinese youths to study abroad.

○ 图6-31　容闳英文回忆
录My Life in China and
America和翻译的多个版本

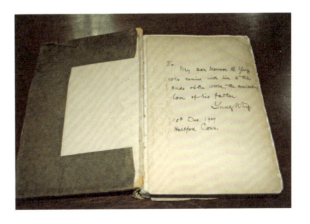

○ 图6-32　容闳送给长子容觐
彤《西学东渐记》，扉页用英
文亲笔题词："给我的儿子
容觐彤。无论他走到世界哪
个地方，都不会失去父亲的
爱。"2010年，容闳之孙容永
成将此书赠给珠海博物馆

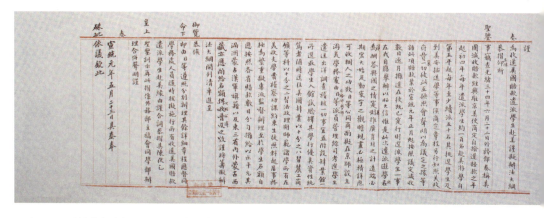

o 图6-33 游美学务处成立后，珠海籍留美幼童唐国安等人负责招考选拔学生。图为《游美学务处呈报本年应送游美学生考试取录办法文》

o 图6-34 第一批庚款学生启程赴美前与唐国安等人合影，其中坐者右一的唐介臣即唐国安，前排站立者左一为当年考试第五名、珠海籍庚款学子唐悦良

（82）1910年/容闳82岁

寓居哈特福德，不幸中风。自知时间不多，加强与孙中山等革命党人的联系。推动荷马·李、布思和孙中山会晤，制定帮助孙中山先生共和革命的资金武器计划，即"中国红龙计划"。

2月14日，孙中山致函容闳，谈及拟向美国银行贷款作为活动经费等事宜；2月16日，致函孙中山，商讨中国红龙计划，提出四条建议：向美国银行贷款150万至200万美元作为起义经费；任用精明能干、熟悉军事的人才统帅军队；组织训练海军；成立领事政府，推举贤能，接管起义后夺取的城市。

留美幼童逐渐走上政治舞台，《纽约时报》以"毕业于本国院校的华人高官"为题，整版报道留美幼童。晚年容闳为幼童们的成就倍感欣慰。"今此百十名学生，强半列身显要，名重一时。"（摘自《西学东渐记》）

1910/at the age of 82

Living in Hartford, Yung Wing unfortunately suffered a stroke. Knowing that his time was limited, he strengthened his ties with revolutionary figures such as Sun Yat-sen. He formulated a plan for providing funds and weapons to assist Dr. Sun's republican revolution, known as the "Chinese Red Dragon Plan."

The CEM students gradually stepped on to the political stage. The *New York Times* devoted an entire page to them.

○ 图6-35　左图为孙中山赠送给容闳推荐的美国军事家荷马·李的题名照。右图为荷马·李

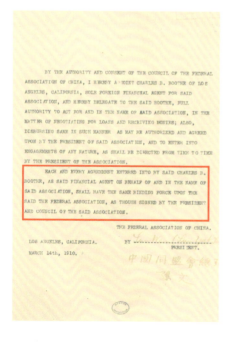

○ 图6-36　左图为孙中山以中国同盟会总理身份授权容闳推荐的美国银行家布思为同盟会对外金融代理人的文件。右图为布思

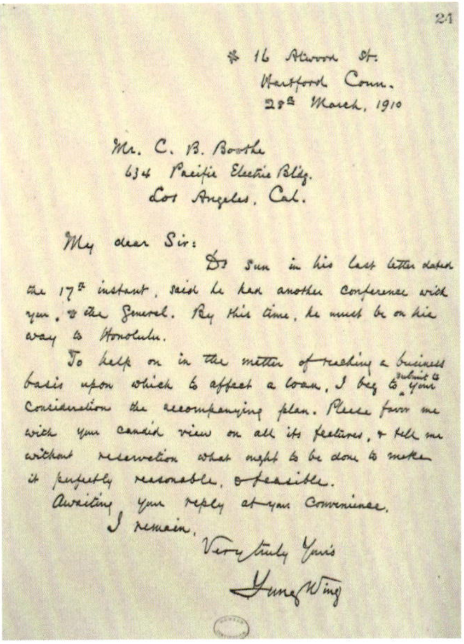

○ 图6-37　左上图为容闳致布思书信手
迹，右上图为孙中山致布思书信手迹，
右下图为荷马·李军事方案手迹

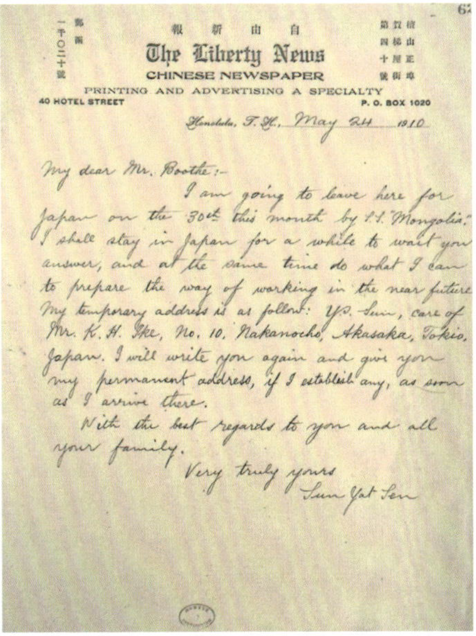

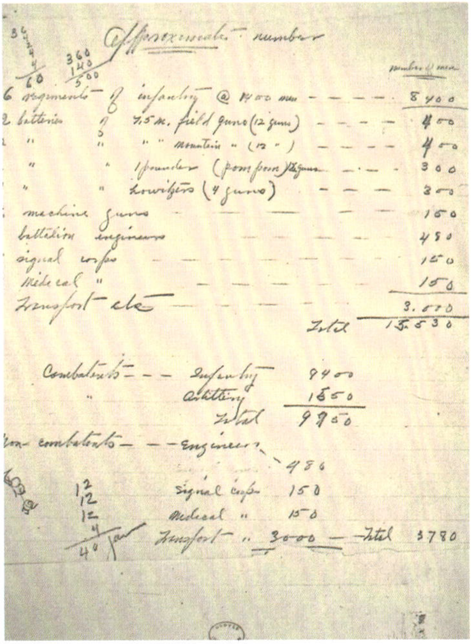

○ 图6-38　《纽约时报》以"毕业于本国院校的中国高官"为题专版报道留美幼童——从左到右依次为唐绍仪、詹天佑、唐元湛、梁诚（上）、罗国瑞（下）、梁如浩、钟文耀、梁敦彦

（83）1911年/容闳83岁

寓居哈特福德，为"中国红龙计划"筹款，与孙中山、美国军事家荷马·李、银行家布思联系频繁。

5月，清廷成立近代中国最早的责任内阁，留美幼童梁敦彦被任命为外务部外务大臣。

是年，孙中山前往哈特福德拜会容闳，因故未能相见。10月10日，辛亥革命爆发。

11月19日，致函中国革命党领导人，告诫他们一定要紧密团结，比兄弟更加亲密。"在任何情况和理由下，你们都不应该互相纠纷，陷入内部争执和内战的深渊。我无需向你们描述无政府状态和混乱的悲惨后果。你们自己知道那是怎样的，自相残杀的战争肯定会导致外国干涉，这就意味着瓜分这个美好的国家。"（摘自容闳《致中国革命党领导人的信》）

12月，唐绍仪作为北方代表与南方革命军代表和平谈判，清朝末代皇帝退位。

是年，幼子容觐槐遵父命回中国报效，后任广东制造局总工程师兼总经理，获授陆军少将军衔。

1911/at the age of 83

Living in Hartford, Yung Wing worked to raise funds for the "Chinese Red Dragon Plan".

On October 10, the Xinhai Revolution broke out, ending the feudal monarchy. Yung Wing wrote a letter to Chinese revolutionaries urging them to obey "the voice of the people" and to immediately organize an interim government.

94

Letter of Invitation to the Leaders or Heads of the following
political Associations of China.

THE PAO WONG WUI or The Chinese Reform Association.
THE KA MING TANG or The Dynastic Change
THE KAO LAO HWUI or The Stalwarts.
THE CHUN CHI WUI or The Independents.

Dear Sir:

I have assurances from responsible parties that a financial
syndicate can be promptly organized to command at once adequate capital
for the sinews of war commensurate with the magnitude of the undertaking;

PROVIDED: That assurances can be given, by the amalgamation
into a single body of the above-mentioned Political Associations in China,
of their intention to unite and so govern themselves as to act harmonious-
ly and as a unit to the end that the old order of things in China may be
changed, that the people may again dwell in peace and that the Empire may
again become powerful.

For us, as individual members, of the great Chinese race, it is
our duty to strive to build up a Chinese Nationality on the broad and
solid principles of unity and solidarity.   To accomplish this object,
every atom and particle of patriotism, and all the noble instincts and
impulses of our nature must be summoned to lay at the altar of our down-
trodden and oppressed country.

For us in a collective capacity as Heads and Leaders of Political Associations, it is our highest and imperative duty to show at this
critical juncture of our National affairs, the utmost forbearance and
patience for each other and drown all our differences, predilictions and
prejudice in order to weld our forces into one compact army and hurl it,
as a concentrated thunder-bolt, against the common enemy.   It is by taking

such a course, both individually and collectively, that we can bring
about the salvation of China and not otherwise.   Strength, power and
might come through cohesion, unanimity and singleness of purpose.   If
we can bring this about China will be ours.

Therefore, I am authorized to invite you to come over as
early and as quickly as possible to Los Angeles, California, for the
purpose of considering all matters bearing upon this subject with the
view of establishing a Grand Council to be composed of the Heads of the
Associations named herein and three members to be designated by the
financial syndicate.   The functions of the Grand Council will be to ar-
range plans, to form a Provisional Government and then to act in an ad-
visory capacity to the Provisional Government when established.

THEREFORE, IT IS IMPERATIVE THAT THE REPRESENTATIVE OF EACH
ASSOCIATION TO THIS CONFERENCE SHALL BE GIVEN FULL DISCRETIONARY POWER
AND AUTHORITY TO DELIBERATE AND ACT AND HIS ACTS MUST BE BINDING UPON
THE OFFICERS AND MEMBERS OF HIS ASSOCIATION IN ALL MATTERS AGREED UPON
BY THE GRAND COUNCIL.

As soon as the Provisional Government is organized, the sum of
one million, five hundred thousand dollars ($1,500,000) (gold) will be
raised at once by the financial syndicate and delivered over to the Treasurer of the Provisional Government.   At the end of from six to twelve months
another sum of $1,500,000 (gold) will be paid and so on.   When the Grand
Council is satisfied that enough funds are raised authority will be given
to begin operations.

On receipt of this communication, you will respond at once,
whether or not you will come.   If you cannot come yourself, you may dele-
gate an accredited and responsible agent with full power to act for you.

Fraternally yours,

Yung Wing

o 图6-39 容闳11月19日致中国革命党领导人的信函，下图为容闳手迹

○ 图6-40 留美幼童、清末皇族内阁成员、外务大臣梁敦彦

○ 图6-41 是年12月，孙中山从美国返抵香港时在船上与欢迎者合影，前排左四为孙中山，左一为与孙中山同船抵达的军事顾问荷马·李

（84）1912年/容闳84岁

寓居哈特福德。1月1日，中华民国临时政府成立，孙中山就任临时大总统。1月2日，致函孙中山表示祝贺："我为能活到看到你当选中华民国第一任总统之日而欣喜。"同日，孙中山致函容闳，邀请他归国辅佐，并附近照一张。"民国建设，在在需才。素仰盛名，播震寰宇，加以才智学识，达练过人，用敢备极欢迎，恳请先生归国，而在此中华民国创立一完全之政府，以巩固我幼稚之共和。临风濡颖，不胜鹄盼之至。"（摘自孙中山致容闳信函）。

4月15日，突发脑溢血。

4月20日，收到孙中山信函及照片，已经处于昏迷状态。

4月21日上午11点30分，在哈特福德沙京街284号离世，享年84岁。

4月22日，《哈城日报》《纽约时报》《哈特福德报》《春田联合报》《耶鲁校友周刊》等美国媒体报道了容闳去世的消息，称他为学者、政治家及今日新中国运动的先驱者。

4月23日，在避难山教堂举行追思会，与爱妻玛丽合葬于哈特福德市西岱山公墓。方基圆顶的墓碑下端，四方形的中文"容"字仿佛在诉说，墓中人虽然客死异邦，但他的心一直眷恋着自己的祖国。

是年，留美预备学校清华学堂更名清华学校（清华大学前身），珠海籍留美幼童唐国安担任首任校长。

珠海籍留美幼童唐绍仪出任首任内阁总理，珠海籍留美幼童梁如浩出任外交总长，珠海籍留美幼童唐元湛出任首任电报总局局长。

是年，珠海籍留美幼童容星桥和族人在南屏筹款重修容闳创办的甄贤学校，永久纪念家乡先贤。学校延续至今，薪火传承百年。

1912/at the age of 84

On January 1, the Provisional Government of the Republic of China was established and Sun Yat-sen assumed office as the Provisional President. He urgently wrote to Yung Wing, inviting him to return to China to assist in the construction of the country.

On April 21, at 11:30 a.m, Yung Wing passed away in Hartford at the age of 84.

That year, CEM student Tong Shao Yi became China's first Prime Minister. Another CEM student Liang Yu Ho became the Foreign Minister, Tong Yuen Chan became the Director of the Telegraph Bureau, and Tong Kwo became the first president of Qinghua School (the predecessor of Tsinghua University).

o 图6-42　1912年1月2日，容闳从美国致函孙中山，祝贺孙中山就任中华民国临时大总统，同时对新建立的共和国政府面临的国际形势以及军队财政等问题提出建议，并推荐耶鲁大学毕业的儿子容觐槐回国效力。图为容闳致孙中山签名信函

o 图6-43　珠海籍留美幼童、中华民国首任内阁总理唐绍仪（右一）和他的内阁成员

○ 图6-44 左图为清华学校首任校长唐国安。右图为清华校园

○ 图6-45 左图为民国首任电报总局局长唐元湛。右图为上海电报局工作场景

○ 图6-46　《警务丛报》1912年第1卷第19期
第2页刊登的容闳遗照

○ 图6-47　《纽约时报》《哈特福德报》《春田联合报》《耶鲁校友周刊》等美国媒体报道了容
闳去世的报道（由左到右）

○ 图6-48 容闳和玛丽在
哈特福德西岱山公墓的合
葬墓

后代及附表

容闳临终之际，寄语孩子"吾费如许金钱，养成汝辈人才，愿冀回报祖国""为共和国效力"。按照父亲的遗愿，两个儿子陆续回到中国。

On the verge of his death, Yung Wing imparted his last words to his children, "I have spent so much money in cultivating talents for our country. I hope that you will repay our motherland by serving the Republic." In accordance with their father's last wishes, his two sons returned to China one after another.

（1）长子容觐彤（Morrison Brown Yung）

　　容觐彤（1876—1933），毕业于耶鲁大学，矿业工程师。1909年按照父亲嘱托回国，参与制定武昌起义后重建汉口的整体规划。1921年，被非常大总统孙中山亲自任命为内务部技师。著有中国第一部《中国矿业条例》草案。葬于香港薄扶林华人基督教坟场，其子容永成现居新加坡。

○ 图7-1　容觐彤证件照和在古巴矿场的持枪照

○ 图7-2　容闳之孙容永成（左三）携家人在香港薄扶林华人基督教坟场拜祭父亲容觐彤

（2）次子容觐槐（Bartlett Golden Yung）

容觐槐（1879—1942），毕业于耶鲁大学，机械工程师。1911年按照父亲嘱托回国，任广东制造局总工程师兼总经理，获授陆军少将军衔；逝于上海。2005年，其长女容文真定居珠海，2009年去世。

○ 图7-3　左图为容闳之孙容永成家中珍藏的容觐槐照片，右图为耶鲁大学馆藏容觐槐照片和档案

○ 图7-4　左图为容觐槐1913年在北京被捕，经留美幼童蔡廷干营救出狱，当时引起了较大的社会反响，《东方杂志》连载了《容觐槐（容闳之子）在华遭际之自述》。中图为容觐槐自述中关于从澳门返回故乡（珠海）夜宿陈芳家宅、拜访唐绍仪的相关记载。右图为容觐槐1914年照片

容毅槐（Bartlett G.Yung）致孙中山
函 （1912年1月2日）

（原文）

Brooklyn, N.Y., January 2nd, 1912.

His Excellency Sun Yat Sen, Shanghai, China.

Dear Sir:

In adding my congratulations to the general chorus, let me volunteer my services to the Republic in any capacity here or in China—qualifications as follows:

Son of Yung Wing; graduate of Yale University, class of 1902; Mechanical Engineer; ten years' practical experience running this manufacturing business; age 32; single; have some connections, acquaintances, and access to bankers in New York City. Have also had three (3) years' military training in Squadron A, Troop I Cavalry N.G.N.Y.—willing to volunteer for the army.

Hoping you can make use of me.

I remain, Very respectfully yours,

Bartlett G.Yung

Dict.BGY/MJ

（译文）

纽约布鲁克林，1912年1月2日

致孙逸仙阁下，中国上海。

尊敬的先生：

谨让我随众齐声祝贺您，并愿以任何身份在此或回国为共和国效力。我的履历如下：

容闳之子，耶鲁大学1902届毕业生，机械工程师，拥有10年制造业管理的实践经验，32岁，未婚。在纽约的银行家中有一些关系。曾在纽约的国民志愿军机动地面部队I班A中队服役三年——愿意为军队服务。

希望为您效劳。

容毅槐 敬上

○ 图7-5　左图为容毅槐证件照，右图为容毅槐1912年1月2日致孙中山先生函

○ 图7-6　容毅槐在上海的墓碑

容闳学历表

时 间	学 校	阶 段
1838—1840	郭士腊夫人女塾（Mrs.Gutzlaff School）	
	小学启蒙	
1841—1847	马礼逊学校（Morrison School）	小学+中学混合制
1847—1850	孟松学校（Monson Academy）	中学预科
1850—1854	耶鲁学院（Yale College）	大学本科

容闳履历表

时 间	职 务
1855	美国驻华公使伯驾秘书
1855—1856	香港高等法院传译员
1856	上海江海关翻译处头等通事
1857—1861	宝顺洋行书记员
1861	琼记洋行九江茶行经纪人
1861—1863.9	自营茶行（江西九江）
1863—1865	曾国藩委办赴美采购机器（五品蓝翎）
1866—1868	曾国藩幕僚（五品花翎运同衔）
1868—1872	江苏巡抚署丁日昌翻译（以同知留于江苏遇缺即补）
1872—1875	出洋肄业局副监督（三品衔江苏候补道）
1878—1882	出使美日秘三国副公使（二品衔江苏候补道）
1895—1896	江南交涉委员（江苏候补道）

容闳自传各版本表

英文版

序 号	书 名	出版社	年 份
1	My life in China and America	NewYork:Henry Holt And Company	1909
2	My life in China and America	New York:Arno Press	1978
3	My life in China and America	美国联合技术公司	1997
4	My life in China and America	太原：山西教育出版社	2002
5	容闳自传：我在中国和美国的生活(中英)	北京：团结出版社	2005

续表

容闳自传各版本表			
英文版			
序　号	书　名	出版社	年　份
6	容闳回忆录：我在中国和美国的生活(中英)	北京：东方出版社	2006
7	My life in China and America	香港：China Economic Review Publishing	2007
8	My life in China and America	香港：China Economic Review Publishing	2008
日文版——百濑弘译 坂野正高解说			
序　号	书　名	出版社	年　份
1	西学东渐记——容闳自传	东京平凡社	1969
中文译本1——徐凤石 恽铁樵译			
序　号	书　名	出版社	年　份
1	西学东渐记——容纯甫先生自述	上海：商务印书馆	1915
2	西学东渐记	上海：商务印书馆	1934
3	西学东渐记	台北：广文书局	1961
4	西学东渐记（容闳自传）	台北：文星书店	1965
5	西学东渐记——容闳自传	东京平凡社	1969
6	西学东渐记——容闳自传（2册）	台北：学人月刊杂志社	1971
7	西学东渐记——容闳自传	台北：文海出版社	1973
8	西学东渐记	台北：广文书局	1977
9	西学东渐记——容纯甫先生自述	武汉：华中师院历史系资料室	不详
10	西学东渐记	台北：广文书局	1981
11	西学东渐记	长沙：湖南人民出版社	1981
12	西学东渐记（合订本）	长沙：湖南人民出版社	1985
13	西学东渐记——容纯甫先生自述	上海：上海书店出版社	1992
14	西学东渐记	美国联合技术公司	1997

中文译本1——徐凤石 恽铁樵译			
序　号	书　名	出版社	年　份
15	中国留学生之父的足迹与心迹——西学东渐记	郑州：中州古籍出版社	1998
16	容闳自传：我在中国和美国的生活（中英文本）	北京：团结出版社	2005
17	西学东渐记	珠海：珠海出版社	2006
18	容闳回忆录：我在中国和美国的生活（中英文本)	北京：东方出版社	2006
19	西学东渐记（合订本）	长沙：湖南人民出版社	2008
20	西学东渐记	北京：生活·读书·新知三联书店	2011
21	西学东渐记——容纯甫先生自叙	广州：新世纪出版社	2011
22	容闳回忆录：我在中国和美国的生活	北京：东方出版社	2012
23	容闳自述	合肥：安徽文艺出版社	2014
24	西学东渐记	长沙：岳麓书社	2015
25	西学东渐记	北京：朝华出版社	2017
中文译本2——王蓁译			
序　号	书　名	出版社	年　份
1	我在美国和在中国生活的追忆	北京：中华书局	1991
2	西学东渐记	北京：中国人民大学出版社	2011
中文译本3——石霓译注			
序　号	书　名	出版社	年　份
1	容闳自传：我在中国和美国的生活	上海：百家出版社	2003
中文译本4——女汉本-王志通 左滕慧子译注			
序　号	书　名	出版社	年　份
1	耶鲁中国人——容闳自传	南京：江苏凤凰出版社	2018

【晚清首批官派留美幼童名录】

（共120名，按生源地域人数排列）

广东省（84人）

今珠海（24人）

蔡绍基	邓士聪	容尚谦	张康仁	谭耀勋	蔡廷干	邓桂廷	黄有章
梁金荣	容尚勤	张有恭	唐国安	唐元湛	卓仁志	梁如浩	唐绍仪
唐致尧	容耀垣	徐振鹏	唐荣浩	唐荣俊	吴其藻	谭耀芳	盛文扬

广东省其他地方（60人）

蔡锦章	程大器	欧阳庚	史锦镛	钟俊成	钟文耀	刘家照	陆永泉
李恩富	李桂攀	宋文翙	郑廷襄	黄耀昌	刘玉麟	陈绍昌	潘铭钟
何廷樑	梁敦彦	黄仲良	陈钜溶	陈荣贵	邝荣光	吴仰曾	曾笃恭
黄开甲	罗国瑞	詹天佑	陈佩瑚	邝景垣	邝詠钟	苏锐钊	梁普时
梁普照	方伯樑	容 揆	温秉忠	吴应科	吴仲贤	曾 溥	徐之煊
邝贤俦	邝景扬	杨兆楠	杨昌龄	曹嘉爵	曹嘉祥	黄季良	林沛泉
卢祖华	周长龄	陈福增	梁金鳌	陶廷赓	潘斯炽	林联辉	林联盛
冯炳忠	梁丕旭	邝炳光	邝国光				

江苏省（含上海，22人）

钱文魁	牛尚周	曹吉福	陆锡贵	张祥和	祁祖彝	朱锡绶	曹茂祥
康赓龄	沈嘉树	周万鹏	朱宝奎	宦维城	陈金揆	沈寿昌	陆德彰
吴焕荣	周传谏	周传谔	朱汝淦	金大廷	王仁彬		

浙江省（8人）

王凤喈	王良登	丁崇吉	陈乾生	孙广明	袁长坤	沈德辉	沈德耀

安徽省（3人）

吴敬荣	程大业	黄祖莲

福建省（2人）

黄锡宝　薛有福

山东省（1人）

石锦堂

【部分幼童任职岗位】

詹天佑	"中国铁路之父"，京张铁路总工程师
唐绍仪	民国首任内阁总理
蔡绍基	北洋大学首任校长
唐国安	清华学校首任校长
梁敦彦	清末外务部尚书
梁如浩	民初外交总长
蔡廷干	北洋政府外交总长、内阁代总理
唐元湛	民国首任电报总局局长
徐振鹏	民初海军部次长
刘玉麟	清末驻英公使
梁丕旭	清末驻美公使
周万鹏	清末全国电政总局局长
周长龄	香港第一位华人行政署议员
张康仁	美国首位华人律师
吴应科	民初海军右司令
黄仲良	津浦铁路总办

钟文耀　　沪宁铁路管理局局长

罗国瑞　　津浦铁路南段总局总办

陆永泉　　中国驻纽约领事

黄开甲　　圣路易斯博览会中国馆副监督

欧阳庚　　中国驻旧金山总领事

容尚谦　　清末"环泰号"军舰舰长

邝荣光　　直隶省矿政调查局总勘矿师

苏锐钊　　中国驻新加坡总领事

梁金荣　　江西电报局局长

吴仲贤　　江汉关监督兼外交部特派湖北交涉员

宋文翙　　湖北军政府海军舰队司令

王良登　　中国驻古巴总领事

容　揆　　中国驻美学生监督

朱宝奎　　上海电报局总办

邝景扬　　津浦等铁路总工程师

程大业　　满洲里电报局局长

卢祖华　　京奉铁路局局长

曹嘉祥　　民初海军次长

容耀垣　中华民国临时政府总统府高等顾问

林联辉　北洋医学堂首任校长

唐荣浩　山东省道台

唐荣俊　上海南京铁路局局长

吴其藻　中国驻朝鲜领事

陶廷赓　湖北电报局局长

丁崇吉　上海江海关副税务司

方伯樑　山海关内外路矿学堂首任监督

袁长坤　交通部电报总局局长

邝国光　湖北省政府外事秘书、上海江南造船厂经理

邝炳光　北洋水师"金鸥号"炮艇指挥

盛文扬　福州电报局局长

温秉忠　暨南学堂首任总理

吴仰曾　国民政府工矿厅工程师

梁普照　开平矿务局船务局帮办

邝祖彝　满洲里安东道台

黄耀昌　京汉铁路总局副局长

袁长坤　交通部电报管理委员会主任

我走过你走过的路

徐惠萍

偌大中国，1995年，我从边陲贵阳东移上千公里来到了珠海，几经搬迁定居在华发新城社区，这里距离容闳故居直线距离不超过400米，都属于一个叫南屏的小镇。当然那个时候是叫做南屏村，容闳的家在村里，我现在的家应该是紧邻村口的荒野，或者田地。夜深人静，我偶尔会想起，容闳小时候曾经走村串寨卖糖果，是不是也会经过了我脚下的这片地。就像现在很火的两句歌词：我吹过你吹过的风，这算不算相拥？我走过你走过的路，这算不算相逢？

这样的想法总会让我有几许激动，我越来越相信，冥冥之中，我和容闳是有约定的。

我曾在另一本书的后记写下过这样一段话："如果说有一个人的精神，像一块磁铁，牢牢地牵引着我的灵魂，让我自觉或不自觉地成为他的追随者，那么这个人就是容闳。"时至今日，我依然觉得这是一段精准的描述。隔着百余年的时空距离，我能感受到他温存的目光和他的鞠躬尽瘁、肝胆披沥。在为他高山仰止的精神唏嘘不已的同时，心里面又会有一种深深的不平，容闳对这个民族的贡献和这个民族对他的记忆落差之大，瞠目结舌。其实大凡真正读懂容闳的人，心里面大多藏着同样的感伤。

中国社会科学院近代史研究所研究员雷颐是中国史学界较早关注容闳的学者之一，他认为容闳是中国全球化进程的先驱。记得十年前和雷教授去珠海电视台做一个关于容闳的节目，电视台的走廊上摆放着几尊珠海名人的雕像，雷颐站在容闳的雕像前，面色凝重，半晌说了这么一句话：我真有一种冲动，想把这个雕像搬到珠海的大广场上。那个时候珠海的公共广场上是没有容闳雕像的。当然现在也基本没有。

2019年世界读书日，著名海归学者施一公先生郑重推荐我和安兴兄的《先行者容闳》，施一公非常敬重容闳，他认为正是容闳实质性地推动晚清科学教育领域的近代化进程，他说如今的每一个学生，如果一代代往上溯源的话，最初的老师都可以说是容闳。然而出乎他意料的是，他在中国演讲，当问起谁知道容闳时，常常黑压压的听众群里，几乎没有人知道容闳是谁。

久仰大名却素未谋面的耶鲁大学苏炜教授百忙中为这本《容闳图传》写序，看到他的序，隔着浩瀚的太平洋，立刻有一种情绪同频共振。一句"愧欠先生三万里"振聋发聩，直击心扉。他这样写："无论从哪一个意义上说，容闳，都是近现代中国史中一个无可忽略也无可替代、留下过深刻足迹的历史巨人。"然而，每每他给造访耶鲁的中国客人讲述容闳之后，那些被震撼了的客人也同样会惊诧：为什么这么有分量的一位历史人物，我们这些受过高等教育的人，更别说一般中国人，却都全然不知晓。

有一位已经仙逝了的长者，对容闳的拳拳之情，天地也为之动容，正是他二十多年前，从耶鲁大学带回了容闳档案的微缩胶卷，开启了对这段尘封历史的系统研究。他就是中国史学界泰斗章开沅先生，2014年89岁的他已经闭门谢客了，却欣然接受我们的采访，中午还要请我们吃饭，说因为你们是为容闳而来，92岁高龄又不辞辛劳为容闳再次来到珠海。他说容闳是最早走出国门睁眼看世界的人，是中国近现代知识分子的标志性人物，对容闳的研究起步较晚，需要加紧深入地发掘。他还说他此生最大的遗憾，就是不能把容闳捐给耶鲁大学的那些中文典籍，一本一本找出来。音容宛在，不甚感怀。

一个人影响一群人，一群人影响一代人，继而影响一个国家的近代化进程。容闳就是这样一个传奇先贤。然而直到今天，容闳的价值依然没有被社会所认识，我在美国国会图书馆查容闳资料的时候，一位北大毕业的图书管理员对我说：容闳像一个悲剧，他为中国做了那么多的事，但是在中国没有几个人记住他。这句话深深地刺痛了我。当然，容闳是不会在乎这些的，他的情怀里面没有"小我"，没有个人得失，只有他的民族、他的国家。但是我在乎，同为珠海人，说出他的故事于我是责任，是使命，也是契约。所以虽然不是历史专业出身，但是10多年来我不曾放弃，始终执着地在他的人生轨迹里，在他的时代进步的轨迹里磕磕碰碰寻找着他的点点滴滴。今天终于完成的这本书，是献给他诞辰195周年最好的礼物。书中难免有疏漏和错误的地方，敬请指正和谅解。

能写出这本书，我要感谢许多的人，感谢那些像雷颐教授那样不厌其烦指导我的大家学者；感谢那些像沈荣国、宾睦新那样有着深厚专业背景的伙伴，有求必应，有问必答；感谢那些像刘建飞、林卫旗、罗杰、李琛、王骁言以及梁凯茵那样的好朋友一次次地为我找资料，校对错误。感谢本书的英文翻译Sam Jake Leong Wong，他是容闳好友、中国第一本英汉词典编撰者邝其照的玄孙，虽然至今我们没有见面，却因为百年前那些遥远的人和事变成了熟悉的朋友。

当然，特别的爱和谢意要给我93岁的母亲，她始终如一地支持我，鼓励我。即便是躺在病床上，她也总是催着我去动笔，她说：看到你写书的背影我就很骄傲，因为我的女儿做的是一件有意义的事。

容闳是珠海的，容闳也是中国的，容闳更是世界的，愿更多的人通过这本中英文的《容闳图传》，了解他的故事，追逐他的梦想，爱之所爱，行之所行，秋水天长，无问西东。

2023年11月20日完稿于珠海南屏华发新城